EVERY DAY IS FOR THE THIEF

Teju Cole

EVERY DAY IS
FOR THE THIEF

With photos by the author

Annotations by Mechthild Hesse

Ernst Klett Sprachen
Stuttgart

1. Auflage   7 | 2025

Alle Drucke dieser Auflage sind unverändert und können im Unterricht nebeneinander verwendet werden.
Die letzte Zahl bezeichnet das Jahr des Druckes. Das Werk und seine Teile sind urheberrechtlich geschützt. Jede Nutzung in anderen als den gesetzlich zugelassenen Fällen bedarf der vorherigen schriftlichen Einwilligung des Verlags.

We would like to thank Maria Benet for permission to reprint three lines from "Three American-Style Studies of a Landscape Rendered Foreign" from *Mapmaker of Absences* (San Francisco, CA. Sixteen Rivers Press, 2005). Used by permission.
Every Day Is for the Thief is a work of fiction. Names, characters, places, and incidents either are the product of the author's imagination or are used fictitiously. Any resemblance to actual persons, living or dead, events, or locales is entirely coincidental.

Worterklärungen von Mechthild Hesse

Redaktion: Debby Böhm
Layoutkonzeption: Sandra Vrabec
Fotos: Teju Cole
Gestaltung und Satz: Joachim Schrimm, bostext, Friolzheim
Umschlaggestaltung: Maja Merz
Titelbild: Getty Images (peeterv), München
Druck und Bindung: Salzland Druck, Staßfurt

Printed in Germany
ISBN 978-3-12-579908-0

*for Karen
and for my parents,
and Jeremy and Bibi*

About the author

Teju Cole was raised in Nigeria and moved to the United States in 1992. He is a writer, photographer and art historian. His novel *Open City* won the PEN/Hemingway Award, the New York City Book Award for Fiction and the *Internationaler Literaturpreis*, and was shortlisted for the National Book Critics Circle Award and the Ondaatje Prize of the Royal Society of Literature. He lives in New York City.

Abbreviations

esp	especially
etc	et cetera (and so on)
inf	informal
pl	plural
sb	somebody
sth	something
usu	usually

The window was one of many,
the town was one. It was the only one,
the one I left behind.

—Maria Benet, *Mapmaker of Absences*

Ojo gbogbo ni t'ole, ojo kan ni t'olohun.
Every day is for the thief, but one day
is for the owner.

—Yoruba proverb

Contents

ONE

I wake up late the morning I'm meant to go to the consulate. As
I gather my documents just before setting out, I call the hospital
to remind them I won't be in until the afternoon. Then I enter
the subway and make my way over to Second Avenue and,
5 without much trouble, find the consulate. It occupies several
floors of a skyscraper. A windowless room on the eighth floor
serves as the section for consular services. Most of the people
there on the Monday morning of my visit are Nigerians, almost
all of them middle-aged. The men are bald, the women
10 elaborately coiffed, and there are twice as many men as there
are women. But there are also unexpected faces: a tall Italian-
looking man, a girl of East Asian origin, other Africans. Each
person takes a number from a red machine as they enter the
dingy room. The carpet is dirty, of the indeterminate color shared
15 by all carpets in public places. A wall-mounted television plays
a news program through a haze of static. The news continues
for a short while, then there is a broadcast of a football match
between Enyimba and a Tunisian club. The people in the room
fill out forms.
20   There are as many blue American passports in sight as green
Nigerian ones. Most of the people can be set into one of three
categories: new citizens of the United States, dual citizens of the
United States and Nigeria, and citizens of Nigeria who are taking
their American children home for the first time. I am one of the
25 dual citizens, and I am there to have a new Nigerian passport
issued. My number is called after twenty minutes. Approaching
the window with my forms, I make the same supplicant gesture
I have observed in others. The brusque young man seated behind
the glass asks if I have the money order. No, I don't, I say. I had

---

10 **elaborately*** with great care and effort – 14 **dingy*** ['dɪn.dʒi] dark and often
dirty – 16 **haze of static** noise produced by electrical disturbances – 18 **Enyimba**
international Nigerian football club – 27 **supplicant** showing that the other person has
power *(unterwürfig als Antragsteller)* – 29 **money order** payment order for a
pre-specified prepaid amount *(Zahlungsanweisung)*

hoped cash would be acceptable. He points to a sign pasted on the glass: "No cash please, money orders only." He has a name tag on. The fee for a new passport is eighty-five dollars, as indicated on the website of the consulate, but it hadn't been
5 clear that they don't accept cash. I leave the building, walk to Grand Central Terminal, fifteen minutes away, stand in line, purchase a money order, and walk the fifteen minutes back. It is cold outside. On my return some forty minutes later, the waiting room is full. I take a new number, make out the money
10 order to the consulate, and wait.

A small group has gathered around the service window. One man begs audibly when he is told to come back at three to pick up his passport:

–Abdul, I have a flight at five, please now. I've got to get back
15 to Boston, please, can anything be done?

There is a wheedling tone in his voice, and the feeling of desperation one senses about him isn't helped by his dowdy appearance, brown polyester sweater and brown trousers. A stressed-out man in stressed-out clothes. Abdul speaks into the
20 microphone:

–What can I do? The person who is supposed to sign it is not here. That's why I said come back at three.

–Look, look, that's my ticket. Abdul, come on now, just look at it. It says five o'clock. I can't miss that flight. I just can't miss
25 it.

The man continues to plead, thrusting a piece of paper under the glass. Abdul looks at the ticket with showy reluctance and, exasperated, speaks in low tones into the microphone.

–What can I do? The person is *not* here. Okay, please go and
30 sit down. I'll see what can be done. But I can't promise anything.

The man slinks away, and immediately several others rise from their seats and jostle in front of the window, forms in hand.

---

6 **Grand Central Terminal** New York train station – 16 **wheedling** persuading, flattering – 17 **dowdy** old-fashioned, plain – 26 **to plead** to beg – 26 **to thrust** to push strongly – 28 **exasperated**˙ annoyed – 31 **to slink** to walk in a way that you are not noticed – 32 **to jostle** to push *(drängeln)*

–Please, I need mine quickly too. Abeg, just put it next to his.

Abdul ignores them and calls out the next number in the sequence. Some continue to pace near the window. Others retake their seats. One of them, a young man with a skyblue cap, rubs
5 his eye repeatedly. An older man, seated a few rows ahead of me, puts his head into his hands and says out loud, to no one in particular:

–This should be a time of joy. You know? Going home should be a thing of joy.

10 Another man, sitting to my right, fills out forms for his children. He informs me that he recently had his passport reissued. I ask him how long it took.

–Well, normally, it's four weeks.

–Four weeks? I am traveling in less than three. The website
15 assures applicants that passport processing takes only a week.

–It should, normally. But it doesn't. Or I should say, it does, but only if you pay the fee for "expediting" it. That's a fifty-five-dollar money order.

–There's nothing about that on the website.

20 –Of course not. But that's what I did, what I had to do. And I got mine in a week. Of course, the expediting fee is unofficial. They are crooks, you see, these people. They take the money order, which they don't give you a receipt for, and they deposit it in the account and they take out cash from the account. That's
25 for their own pockets.

He makes a swift pulling motion with his hands, like someone opening a drawer. It is what I have dreaded: a direct run-in with graft. I have mentally rehearsed a reaction for a possible encounter with such corruption at the airport in Lagos. But to
30 walk in off a New York street and face a brazen demand for a bribe: that is a shock I am ill-prepared for.

–Well, I'll insist on a receipt.

---

1 **abeg** maybe – 17 **to expedite** to rush, to make sth. happen more quickly –
22 **crook** ˙ criminal – 28 **graft** *here:* corruption – 30 **brazen** ˙ shameless, obvious –
31 **bribe** ˙ *Bestechung*

–Hey, hey, young guy, why trouble yourself? They'll take your money anyway, and they'll punish you by delaying your passport. Is that what you want? Aren't you more interested in getting your passport than in trying to prove a point?

5 Yes, but isn't it this casual complicity that has sunk our country so deep into its woes? The question, unspoken, hangs in the air between me and my interlocutor. It isn't until past eleven that my number is finally called. The story is exactly as he has put it to me. There is an expediting fee of fifty-five dollars in addition 10 to the actual eighty-five dollars that the passport costs. The payment has to be in two separate money orders. I leave the building for the second time that morning, to go and buy another money order. I walk quickly, and am exhausted by the time I return at a quarter to twelve, fifteen minutes before the closing 15 of the window. This time, I don't take a number. I barge my way to the window and submit my form with the required fees. Abdul tells me to pick my passport up in a week. He gives me a receipt only for the original fee. I take it mutely, fold it up, and put it in my pocket. On my way out, next to the elevators, there's a 20 partially torn sign that reads: "Help us fight corruption. If any employee of the Consulate asks you for a bribe or tip, please let us know."

There is no number or email address appended to the note. In other words, I can inform the consulate only through Abdul 25 or one of his colleagues. And it's unlikely that they are the only ones on the take. Perhaps thirty or thirty-five dollars of the "expediting fee" is going to someone over Abdul's head. I catch the look on Abdul's face as I exit the room. He is absorbed in assisting other applicants. It is a farce, given a sophisticated–"no 30 cash please"–sheen.

---

6 **woe**° misery – 7 **interlocutor** person involved in a conversation *(Gesprächspartner, Gegenüber)* – 15 **to barge** to push – 18 **mute**° wordless – 26 **to be on the take** to accept a bribe – 30 **sheen** appearance, surface *(Anschein)*

TWO

It is early evening when the aircraft approaches the low settlements outside the city. It drops gently and by degrees toward the earth, as if progressing down an unseen flight of stairs. The airport looks sullen from the tarmac. It is named for
5 a dead general, and is all that is worst about the architecture of the seventies. With its shoddy white paint and endless rows of small windows, the main building resembles a low-rent tenement. The Air France Airbus touches down and glides onto the tarmac. Relief enters the holds and cabin with the inward-
10 rushing air. Some of my fellow passengers break into applause. Soon, we are trooping out of the craft. A woman weighed down with bags tries to barge through the aisle. "Wait for me," she cries out to her travel companion, loud enough for everyone to hear, "I'm coming." And I, too, experience the ecstasy of arrival,
15 the irrational sense that all will now be well. Fifteen years is a long time to be away from home. It feels longer still because I left under a cloud.

Disembarkation, passport control, and baggage claim eat up more than an hour of our time. The sky outside fills with shadows.
20 One man argues with a listless customs official about the inefficiency.

–This is an international airport. Things should be better run. Is this the impression visitors should have of our nation?

The official shrugs, and says that people like him should return
25 home and make it better. While we wait for the luggage machine to disgorge the bags, a white man next to me makes small talk. He has a brogue, and I ask if he is Scottish. "Aye," he says, and he informs me that he works on the rigs.

---

4 **sullen** hostile – 4 **tarmac** asphalt – 6 **shoddy** cheap – 8 **tenement** ['ten.ə.mənt] apartment building – 20 **listless** lethargic – 27 **brogue** accent – 28 **rig** oil drilling platform

–Got drunk in Paris last night, and got robbed. Firkin' frogs lifted me credit card. But the Champs-Élysées was something! Aye, pissed out me mind. Skunk drunk.

He grins. His teeth are studded with metal. He wears an earring
5 and sports a ginger-tinged five-o'clock shadow. He is not Europe's finest, but he'll earn well here.

–Won't get a flight to Port Harcourt till tomorrow. Staying at the Sheraton tonight. That's where the air hostesses stay, if you get me drift.

10 I nod. My bags finally arrive, damp and streaked with dirt. I lift them onto a cart. On the way out, an official in mufti motions me to stop. He is seated to the side of the door, and doesn't really appear to have any actual function. He's just there. He asks if I am a student. Well, yes, sort of. I figure the lie will speed things
15 along.

–Eh ehn, I thought so. You have that student look. And where do you study?

NYU, I say, the answer that would have been correct three years ago. He nods.

20 –Well, in New York, they spend dollars. You know, dollars.

A meaningless silence passes between us. Then, sotto voce, and in Yoruba, his demand:

–*Ki le mu wa fun wa?* What have you brought for me for Christmas? Because, you know, they spend dollars in New York.

25 I have brought only resolve. I ignore him and roll my bags out to where Aunty Folake and her driver wait for me. When we

---

5 **ginger-tinged five-o'clock shadow** darkness (or here redness) on a man's face caused by the growth of facial hair during the day – 7 **Port Harcourt** largest city of Rivers State; after coal, crude oil was discovered in 1956 and the economy turned to petroleum. Big oil firms have offices in the city. – 8 **if you get me drift** *infm.* if you understand what I mean – 11 **mufti** civilian clothes – 11 **to motion** to make a sign, to indicate – 18 **NYU** New York University – 21 **sotto voce** under his breath, in a quiet voice – 22 **Yoruba** language spoken by one of the three largest ethnic groups of Nigeria – 25 **resolve** * determination

unlock from our embrace, there are tears in her eyes. A scene
out of the prodigal son. She hugs me again and laughs heartily.

–You haven't changed at all! How is that possible?

Outside, the airport looks finer, more regal than it did on
5   approach. The entrances are clogged with passengers' relatives
and, in far greater number, touts, hustlers, and all sorts of people
who are there because they have nowhere else to be.

2 **prodigal son** one of the parables of Jesus (Luke 15:11–32) *(Der verlorene Sohn)* –
4 **regal** ['riːgᵊl] noble – 6 **tout** vendor

19

THREE

On the way home from the airport, at the roundabout of Ikeja
bus stop, where the late afternoon rush makes the traffic snarl,
we come to a complete standstill. Not more than twenty yards
away from us, under the overpass, two policemen bicker. "Go
5   away," one yells at his partner. "Why you always dey stand here?
Why you no go stand that side?" He points to the far side of the
roundabout. For a moment, it seems as if the other officer sees
the sense in the suggestion, but he is slow about carrying it out
because the disagreement has by now attracted stares from
10 pedestrians. He is reluctant to lose face. Both men are slim and
dark, in gray-black uniforms, with machine guns slung over their
shoulders. They stand confused and silent like a pair of actors
who have forgotten their lines. A crowd of commuters gawks at
them from a safe distance.
15   Aunty Folake explains what is going on. Policemen routinely
stop drivers of commercial vehicles at this spot to demand a
bribe. The officer being told off has drifted too close to his
colleague's domain. Such clustering is bad for business: drivers
get angry if they are charged twice. All this takes place under a
20 billboard that reads "Corruption Is Illegal: Do Not Give or Accept
Bribes."
    And how much of the government's money, I wonder, was
siphoned off by the contractor who landed the contract for those
billboards?
25   It is one thing to be told of the "informal economy" of Lagos,
and quite another to see it in action. It puts pressure on
everybody. Some fifteen minutes before we reached Ikeja bus
stop, we had passed a toll gate on Airport Road. It, too, was in
the shadow of a large billboard condemning corrupt practices

---

1 **Ikeja** capital of Lagos State, Nigeria – 4 **to bicker** to argue – 13 **to gawk** to
stare – 20 **billboard** ˙ big advertising board – 23 **to siphon off** to take away
(*abschöpfen*)

and urging citizens to improve the country. The toll at the booth was set at two hundred naira: this was advertised and understood. However, enterprising drivers, such as ours, know that they can get through the toll gate if they pay just half of that. The catch is that the hundred naira they pay goes straight into the collector's purse. "Two hundred you get ticket stub," our driver says, "one hundred you get no ticket. What do I need ticket for? I don't need ticket!" And in this way, thousands of cars over the course of a day would pay the toll at the informal rate, lining the pockets of the collectors and their superiors. The demand from the immigration officer, the Ikeja police, the toll booth story: I encounter three clear instances of official corruption within forty-five minutes of leaving the airport.

Even before I get home that night, though, I see other ways of thinking about these exchanges of money. We stop at Ogba to buy bread. Ogba is some way past Ikeja, at the end of Agidingbi Road. On the way into the shop a doorman salutes us and holds the door open. When we leave the building a few minutes later, he follows us for twenty yards as we move toward the car, and asks for a tip. It is not a demand: it is soft. He does it with the gentleness of someone explaining something to a child.

–Do you have anything for me, sir?

He wears an off-white security guard's uniform and carries no weapon. When my aunt shakes her head, he shakes his head apologetically, smiles, and melts away. When we get to the car, a thin woman in tattered *buba* and *iro* approaches us and says she wants some money for transportation to get home. I don't see her approach, actually; she is just suddenly there, in front of me. She is small and looks ill. A small woman without a name: she is a part of what lies behind the gleaming merchant banks, the posh eateries, the luxury cars. The people who are suddenly there, the many who live off these small gifts.

2 **Naira** currency of Nigeria, 400 naira = ~1 € – 6 **stub** part of a ticket – 9 **to line** *here:* to fill – 26 **tattered buba and iro** torn women's clothing (blouse and wrapper)

Night descends with no warning. I am breathing the air of the city for the first time in a decade and a half, its white smoke and ocher dust which are as familiar as my own breath. But other things, less visible, have changed. I have taken into myself some
5 of the assumptions of life in a Western democracy–certain ideas about legality, for instance, certain expectations of due process– and in that sense I have returned a stranger. What the trip back from the airport makes me think, and what is confirmed over the course of the following days, is the extent to which Lagos
10 has become a patronage society.

Money, dished out in quantities fitting the context, is a social lubricant here. It eases passage even as it maintains hierarchies. Fifty naira for the man who helps you back out from a parking spot, two hundred naira for the police officer who stops you for
15 no good reason in the dead of night, ten thousand for the clearing agent who helps bring your imported crate through customs. For each transaction, there is a suitable amount that helps things on their way. No one else seems to worry, as I do, that the money demanded by someone whose finger hovers over the trigger of
20 an AK-47 is less a tip than a ransom. I feel that my worrying about it is a luxury that few can afford. For many Nigerians, the giving and receiving of bribes, tips, extortion money, or alms–the categories are fluid–is not thought of in moral terms. It is seen either as a mild irritant or as an opportunity. It is a way of getting
25 things done, neither more nor less than what money is there for.

Cash has to change hands, that's the way of the world. Only in excessive cases, like that of the recently convicted inspector general of police, is it viewed as a blight on the system. Tafa

6 **due process** requirement that a state must respect a person's legal rights –
10 **patronage** * the support or influence of a rich and influential person – 12 **lubricant** oil used to make sth work smoothly *(Schmiere)* – 16 **crate** large box used for transport – 20 **AK-47** automatic gun, officially known as the Avtomat Kalashnikova – 20 **ransom** payoff, money paid to receive sth or sb back that was taken *(Lösegeld)* – 22 **extortion** * blackmail – 22 **alms** * donations *(Almosen)* – 29 **blight** disease

Balogun's stolen billions deprived many policemen of their livelihood, and this is part, though not all, of the reason they in their turn extort drivers. Yet, the complaint that most people have is not that Balogun stole money. That a high-ranking
5 government official would embezzle public funds is a given. What annoys people is that he stole so much so quickly. The reasoning was that if only he had shown some moderation, taking only a little here and there, he would not have been arrested. The Balogun case is one of the very few brought against
10 a senior official since the national anticorruption campaign began; the day after my arrival in Lagos, the case is concluded. Balogun is found guilty and given six months in jail for the estimated fourteen billion naira he stole. Six months, that is, for a little over a hundred million dollars. There's no reason, though,
15 for believing that his is the most severe instance of theft. People assume that corruption goes on even at the highest levels of government: contracts, payoffs, oil bunkering. Later, there are rumors in the papers that Tafa Balogun has died in prison. How, why, or when, nobody seems to know. No one seems to mind
20 that he is dead. And when the rumors turn out later to be untrue, that news, too, is met with a shrug.

Most police officers earn between ten and fifteen thousand naira a month. They cannot quite survive on such salaries, which amount to less than one hundred dollars. A friend of my uncle's,
25 an immigration officer, was once transferred out of state and to a remote area of the country. His refusal to take bribes was affecting his colleagues' earnings and, by extension, their ability to provide for their families; he had to be sent somewhere where he would be less of a nuisance. Salaries are similarly low in the
30 armed forces, where, also, there is never any guarantee there will be payment. And it is these heavily armed and poorly paid men who are entrusted with the work of protecting the citizenry.

---

1 **to deprive** to steal, to take away (by force) – 3 **to extort** to force to give –
5 **to embezzle** to steal *(veruntreuen)* – 21 **shrug** (of shoulders) *Schulterzucken* –
29 **nuisance** annoyance, troublemaker

The informal economy is the livelihood of many Lagosians. But corruption, in the form of piracy or of graft, also means that most people remain on the margins. The systems that could lift the majority out of poverty are undercut at every turn. Precisely
5 because everyone takes a shortcut, nothing works and, for this reason, the only way to get anything done is to take another shortcut. The advantage in these situations goes to the highest bidders, those individuals most willing to pay money or to test the limits of the law.
10 A few minutes after I finally arrive at my aunt and uncle's house, the electricity goes out. For those who live here, this sudden deprivation is no surprise. It is a nocturnal ritual. But I'm no longer used to it, and I pass the night fitfully, tracing the shadows that flicker tirelessly on the concrete walls. The air is
15 hot, and thick with old ghosts, and with the smell of kerosene.

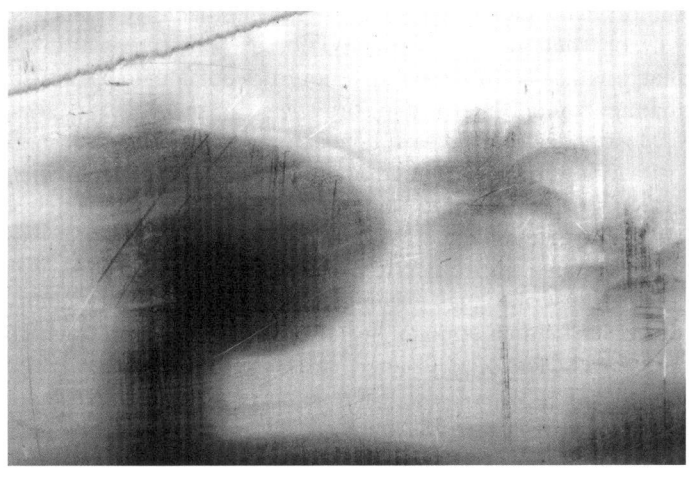

3 **margin** • edge (of society) (*Rand* (*der Gesellschaft*)) – 12 **deprivation** removal, withdrawal (*Entbehrung, Entzug*) – 13 **fitful** • restless

FOUR

A gentle music rouses me the next morning: the muezzin's call
to prayer floating across the forested valley that separates the
house from the minaret. I rise and pad through the house.
Everyone else–my uncle and aunt, my cousins, the servant–is
still asleep. The electricity has not been restored yet. Natural
light leaks into the living room. I make tea. Cockerels' crows,
from another direction, skitter over the muezzin's Arabic. A smell
of cooking smoke arrives from the distance.

From the back porch of the house is a view into a gorge. The
view used to amaze me when I visited this house in the past,
and while I was away my thoughts would periodically wander
over to it. The gorge is now far from pristine. Trees have been
cut down, and tracts of land have been carved out for houses.
Ugly buildings in various stages of completion now loom out of
it. Clinging to the houses like barnacles are white satellite
television dishes. Farther away is a half-built evangelical
megachurch. It is a losing battle for the forest. But it is only
daybreak, and all is as yet tranquil. I stand on the porch drinking
my tea. Viewed from a certain angle, the gorge can still look
primeval, can still conform to a certain idea of Africa: no gasoline
fumes, no gleaming skyscrapers, no six-lane highways. Africa as
bush and thicket. The morning sky is restless. Dark clouds gather
in clumps and, little by little, the clumps gradually disappear.
Light traces silver lines across the wide sky. I finish my tea and
go back inside.

---

3 **to pad** to walk quietly – 7 **to skitter** to move quickly – 9 **gorge** [gɔːrdʒ] deep and
narrow valley – 12 **pristine** [prɪˈstiːn] untouched, new – 14 **to loom out** to appear –
15 **barnacles** shells attaching themselves to the bottom of boats – 20 **primeval**
[prɑiˈmiːvᵊl] ancient, very old – 22 **thicket** area where bushes and trees grow very
closely together (*Dickicht*)

The hallways of the house are bigger than they used to be. The floor is broad and covered with curiously soft white tiles. It is as though I have shrunk in the years since I was last here, or the house itself has gently expanded in the heat, increasing by
5   small amounts in each month of my absence to reach these dimensions. The doorframe is wide and high enough for a family of acrobats to walk through in formation. And there they suddenly are, in my presence, standing on each other's shoulders, their limbs in astral shape. They negotiate the
10 opening, thread it.

The house, of course, is unchanged. It is smaller only in memory. Memory and the intervening years, many of which I have spent in cramped English flats and American apartments, limitations I have endured like a prince in exile. Now, in the cool
15 interior of this great house in Africa, proper size is restored. No single body could dominate a room in such a house. Even the bathroom dwarfs me. I pass through the door that connects the family room to the passageway time and again, as though to test the portal. And each time, I find its generosity marvelous.

20 Part of this story has been told before: the broad doorway, the acrobats. These are incidents from a book I love. Incidents, to be exact, from a dream in that book. But is it any less real to me now for having once happened to someone else elsewhere? For having been recorded in print in the dream, twenty-five years
25 ago, of a great writer returning to his ancestors' Sri Lanka? This is my story now, not his. I am in my aunt's house, but I make it a substitute for that other house of vanished histories, my

3 **to shrink (shrunk, shrunk)** to get smaller – 9 **limb** [lɪm] arm or leg – 13 **cramped** without enough space – 14 **to endure** to bear – 17 **to dwarf** [dwɔːrf] to make sth or sb seem much smaller – 20 **this story** allusion to *Running in the Family* by Michael Ondaatje

demolished childhood home. I gape at the soaring ceiling and look down again, just in time to see the smallest of the acrobats restore her grip. The human star is preserved.

---

1 **to gape** to stare – 1 **soaring** * rising

FIVE

One sign of the newly vital Nigerian economy, and one of the most apparent, is the proliferation of Internet cafes. There had been none when I left home. Now there are several in every neighborhood, and there must be hundreds in Lagos alone. The
5 Internet cafe is symbolic of a connection to goings-on in the larger world, an end to Nigeria's isolation. It is a connection shared by many other large countries trying to shake off poverty. The availability of computers is, in this sense, an index of progress. But while India is an emerging software player, and
10 countries like China, Indonesia, and Thailand have successfully staked claims in manufacturing, Nigeria's contribution is much more modest. In fact it is, for now, limited to the repetition of a single creative misuse of the Internet: advance fee fraud.

The fraud, popularly known as "419" after the section of the
15 Nigerian criminal code it contravenes, is endemic in Nigeria. I have only guessed at the extent of the scam from being on the receiving end of emails which promise a large share of one fund or another in exchange for a small advance fee. I have also read in the American press about people who have been taken in by
20 these offers. My perspective on 419 changes on the morning after I arrive in Lagos. That is when I pay a visit to Tomsed Cyber Cafe near the Ojodu bus stop, some fifteen minutes' walk from my aunt's place. Tomsed is on the second floor of a building that offers print, phone, and fax services. The main computer room
25 is fluorescent-lit and air-conditioned, and it contains twenty-four machines, all connected to the Internet by dial-up service. It costs one hundred naira–about seventy cents–to browse for

---

2 **proliferation** ˙ spreading quickly – 11 **to stake a claim** ˙ *einen Platz beanspruchen* –
13 **advance fee fraud** *Vorschussbetrügereien;* **advance fee** *Kreditbeschaffungsprovision;*
The most common email cheat prevalent in the worldwide web are phishing, advance
fee scams and bogus foreign lotteries. – 15 **code** law – 15 **to contravene** to disregard –
16 **scam** ˙ illegal plan for making money (often involving tricks) – 19 **to be taken in** to
step into a trap *(auf etw. hereinfallen)*

an hour. This cost, even in the absence of a regulatory body, is remarkably consistent at Internet cafes of different standards across the city. Of at least seven I end up visiting, none costs significantly more or less than Tomsed does.

5   The cafe is close to capacity. Most of the customers are young men with a certain look: close-cropped hair, lean faces. They are dressed in short-sleeved shirts, and all of them are over twenty and under forty. After paying the attendant, I take a seat and wait for the Internet page to load. The man seated next to

10 me composes a message by the hunt and peck method. He presses one letter on the keyboard, searches for the next, presses that one, and so on. It is his one-fingered technique that attracts my attention, but when my eye alights, not entirely accidentally, on his text, I catch my breath. The words I see him type, "transfer,"

15 "dear friend," "deposited into your account forthwith," present incontrovertible evidence: he is composing a 419 letter. I have stumbled onto the origin of the world-famous digital flotsam.

    I feel as though I have discovered the source of the Nile or the Niger. The man keeps at his typing with the single-mindedness

20 of a hen picking a yard clean. Above him, on the wall of the cybercafe, is a large yellow sign with black block letters that warns: "TO OUR CUSTOMERS–Tomsed Cyber Cafe now has an activity monitor software that monitors all activities of 419s including their mails in all our workstations. Therefore any

25 customer caught with 419 job will be handed over to the police. BE WARNED!" The man knows the risks, but he carries on nonetheless, casting his net out into the unknown, prompted by urgings so frequently indulged that they have become instinctive. Later, I see other men with the same shifty faces, all

30 of them composing letters or using the chat features of Yahoo

---

2 **consistent** *here:* the same – 5 **close to capacity** almost full – 6 **lean** thin – 13 **to alight** to land on – 16 **incontrovertible** undeniable, definite – 16 **evidence** proof – 17 **flotsam** unwanted or unimportant object or person *(Treibgut)* – 27 **nonetheless** *here:* despite the warning *(nichtsdestotrotz)* – 28 **urging** desire – 28 **to indulge** to allow to have, to accept *(nachgeben, (sich) Wünsche erfüllen)*

and Microsoft to reel in their victims. After I see several such incidents at Tomsed, the initial frisson I felt disappears and is replaced by irritation.

I ask my cousin Muyiwa what he knows about the practice.
5 He informs me that the universities, the one he attends in Osun State included, are the nerve centers of this activity. For most of the boys, the goal is to get cash so they can live large and impress their mates on campus. They call the scam "nineteen" (a further abbreviation of 419), and they themselves are known
10 as "the yahoo boys" or simply "yahoo yahoo." While they often work in daytime, they prefer the night: that is when they have discounts at the cafes. Under cover of night, the yahoo yahoo can work for long, coffee-fueled stretches, unmolested by censors.

15 Yahoo yahoo are on the front lines of their own shadow war, mangling what little good name their country still has. Their successes depend on the gullibility of foreigners, who apparently are still in plentiful supply. There is a sense, I think, in which the swindler and the swindled deserve each other. It is a kind
20 of mutual humiliation society. Once, looking to my right in an Internet cafe–and this surreptitious reading quickly becomes habitual for me–I see a letter being written from the "Chairman of the National Office for Petroleum Resources." The writer is a rough-looking man who is clearly chairman of nothing. There
25 are other letters, from the heirs of fictional magnates, from the widows of oil barons, from the legal representatives of incarcerated generals, and they are such enterprising samples of narrative fiction that I realize Lagos is a city of Scheherazades.

---

1 **to reel in** to catch – 2 **frisson** short moment of emotional excitement – 3 **irritation*** anger – 13 **to molest*** to bother – 16 **to mangle** to destroy – 17 **gullability** naiveté – 20 **mutual*** shared – 21 **surreptitious** done secretly, subtle – 25 **heir** [er] *Erbe* – 27 **to incarcerate*** to imprison – 27 **sample*** example – 28 **Scheherazade** [ʃə,hɜrə'zɑːdə] storyteller and main female character in *One Thousand and One Nights*

The stories unfold in ever more fanciful iterations and, as in the myth, those who tell the best stories are richly rewarded.

Long email lists are cut from one page and pasted on another. The men work words with the intensity and focus of dowsers,
5 leading their readers down fanciful paths, persuading them with barely concealed desperation. The nets are cast and cast again, because were there to be even a single bite, were there just one victim, the many hours spent staring into the glowing screen would have been worth it, the risk of being caught by the police
10 would have been justified. An advance fee of ten thousand dollars can leave a yahoo yahoo set for months; many of them angle for much bigger payoffs than that. The engine for this industry is greed, and it is impossible to control because it is far more decentralized than anyone can govern. All this somehow
15 reminds me of *Gulliver's Travels,* which I read when I was a schoolboy in Lagos. In his fourth and final journey, Lemuel Gulliver's preference for the company of the horselike Houyhnhnms comes at the expense of a race of uncouth creatures. Swift names this latter group, who were rather too
20 close to humans for Gulliver's liking, "the Yahoos." It is a neat reversal of Marx's dictum about history: the yahoo yahoo have bucked a trend, showing up the first time as farce and the second, in Nigeria, as something more tragic.

Nigerian law enforcement agents do what they can to battle
25 the yahoo yahoo. In addition to the warning signs that are posted at every cafe, there is often a policeman or a soldier hanging about the entrance of the cafe. At Tomsed, the soldier in front

---

1 **iteration** repetition – 4 **dowser** person who uses a divining rod *(Wünschelrute)* –
6 **concealed** hidden – 15 **Gulliver's Travels** title of a satirical novel by Jonathan Swift
(1726) – 18 **at the expense of** auf Kosten von – 18 **uncouth** [ʌnˈkuːθ] vulgar,
uncivilized – 21 **Marx** Karl Marx (1818–1883) German philosopher and political
economist after whom Marxism, a form of communism, is named. His dictum is: "From
each according to his ability, to each according to his needs." – 22 **to buck a trend** to
behave differently to general development

of me caresses his tommy gun and cracks jokes with the staff, while the men to my left and right are busy with their fraudulent work. I ask Muyiwa about arrests, and he says it is actually quite common to see an officer hauling off a yahoo yahoo. They drag
5 them outside and, threatening them with incarceration and torture, are able to exact steep fines, fifty thousand naira, say, which is more than three hundred dollars. This goes straight into the pockets of the arresting officers. It is a catch and release program. The yahoo yahoo, naturally, promise themselves to be
10 more careful the next time. They find another Internet cafe, and get right back to work.

---

1 **to caress** to stroke, to pat – 1 **tommy gun** machine gun – 6 **to exact steep fines** ˙ *hohe Geldstrafen einfordern*

SIX

One morning, a child comes into the broad corridor of the house
and greets me. I am shaving, unprepared for a guest. She calls
me by name, and tells me who she is. We have never laid eyes
on each other but we recognize each other immediately: first
cousins. She was born after I left home, the last daughter of my
father's younger brother and, until this moment, we have only
been rumors to each other. But so quickly do we get to know
each other that, soon, I cannot even remember a time when I
did not know her. *She moved so easily all I could think of was*
sunlight. We spend hours on the sofa watching television. She
teaches me about all the new films and the biggest music stars.
I have brought some chocolates and a knapsack for her, so we
almost have a fair exchange. I am awed by her silences and
excited speech, her darkness, her self-possession. The
completeness of a child is the most fragile and most powerful
thing in the world. A child's confidence is the world's wonder.

A month later, as I prepare to leave, she says she will miss me.
And I know I will miss her too, and I see with a pang that every
good thing I wish for this country, I secretly wish on her behalf.
Any prayer I have that the future be a good one, that the place
keep from breaking, is for her sake.

---

12 **knapsack** backpack – 13 **awed** ˚ overwhelmed, feeling of great respect

SEVEN

My aunt thinks it is a bad idea. Her brother, my Uncle Bello, agrees. Her husband is indifferent, but he acts as if it is a bad idea. Everyone says I must not travel by danfo. The danfo is a death trap. It is a haven for practitioners of black magic, and is
5 full of thieves. This much is known.

–But I used to ride the danfo frequently in my high school days, I even used to ride the molue, which is bigger and more dangerous.

–Ehn, that was a long time ago. You're not quite as hardened
10 now. Yes, you are street-smart, no one doubts it. But like it or not, America has softened you.

Uncle Tunde, Aunty Folake's husband, is amused by the idea that I want to go out and take public transportation. He does it from time to time, sure, but he is not visiting from America. To
15 him and his wife, this is more evidence of my eccentricity. Why not just wait till the next day, so that the driver can take me? My destination is so far and the journey so complicated that any number of things could go wrong. They don't understand that being there on the danfo, being there on the streets, is the whole
20 point of the exercise. And there is no instinct there for helping them understand it, and all they have to hold on to is how contrary I was even as a child, in those years before my father died.

Just as I am about to leave, a guest arrives. He is a young man,
25 the husband of Uncle Tunde's cousin. My aunt asks him if he has a car. He does. In the blink of an eye, she persuades him to drive me all the way to Lagos Island. I know what this is about. It is about keeping the lines of privilege taut. Everyone does it. Each person knows how to get maximum comfort out of
30 situations, how to avoid being "one of the masses." It is essential,

---

3 **danfo** public bus – 4 **haven** ['heɪ.vᵊn] place of safety, refuge *(Zufluchtsort)* – 28 **taut** tight, firm *(straff gespannt)*

not just in terms of safety, but also in social terms. Aunty Folake has not been on a public bus in more than twenty-five years and, as she put it to me: "I'd rather not travel at all, than ever ride in one of those things!" I almost give in, but then it all strikes

5   me as wrong-headed, and I say:

–Wait. This guy has plans of his own. Look, I'll be fine. Why take someone else so far out their way? A guest calls and, next thing, we make him a chauffeur?

My protest settles it. I walk out of the housing estate and

10 within a few minutes find myself in the thick of that assault to the senses that is the Ojodu–Berger Bus Terminus. It is just shy of 9:30 in the morning and the place is teeming. The degree to which my family members wish me to be separate from the life of the city is matched only by my desire to know that life. The

15 danfo, carrier of the masses, is the perfect symbol of our contest. The energies of Lagos life –creative, malevolent, ambiguous– converge at the bus stops. There is no better place to make an inquiry into what it was I longed for all those times I longed for home.

20 The typical Lagos danfo is yellow and decrepit, and seats fourteen: two in front with the driver, and three rows of four passengers each. The bus is operated by a team of two: the driver and a conductor, who is also known as the tout. In the typical bus terminus, such as those at Ojota, Yaba, Ikeja, or Ojodu, the

25 air is thick with the cries of touts. They have to fill those fourteen seats as quickly as possible, and get a move on to their destination. "Jotajota-jotajota." That's the man calling Ojota. "Kejakejakeja. Kejakejastraight." That's the express to Ikeja bus stop. The sound that rises from the thrum of congested traffic

30 is like a chorus of cantors or auctioneers. "Balende–CMS, Balende–CMS, Balende-balende-balende."

---

11 **shy of** *here:* just before – 12 **teeming** very busy – 16 **malevolent** [məˈlevələnt]* mean, nasty, evil – 17 **to converge*** to come together – 20 **decrepit*** falling apart – 29 **congested traffic*** traffic jam – 30 **CMS** Christian Missionary Society located in Lagos Island

Touting is not a job. It is a way of being in the world, a distillate of pure attitude: the chest puffed out, the body limber, the jaw set to brook no opposition. There is in every tout the same no-nonsense attitude, the quick temper, the willingness to get into
5 a fight over any and all conflicts. There is a strut they do, a swagger. These are the original wiseguys of Lagos; some of them are as young as fourteen. They do not go home in the evening and stop being touts. The thing is bound to their souls. The regular non-tout Lagosian, too, has to share this attitude. The
10 body language as one moves through the street has to be one of undiluted self-assurance. Uncertainty in the face or gait attracts attention, and attention is bad. When you catch a stranger's eye, the message you send has to be unequivocal: "Trust me, you don't want to mess with me." There are many
15 people on these streets who roam around looking for victims. People who, through long practice, can sniff out weakness wherever it is.

My Uncle Bello, a well-built man in his forties, told me about going to Oshodi market and being accosted. A rough-looking
20 man approached him on the Oshodi overpass and asked for money. My uncle thought about it and gave him two hundred naira. The man was unimpressed.

–Ah, no o. My money is one thousand.

Uncle Bello said he had to assess at that point whether to call
25 the guy's bluff or to cave in to the extortion. He called his bluff. It was a bad move. The guy got extremely hostile.

–Heh? What do you mean by no? I will waste you. I will waste you. You see this bridge? I'll dangle you from the edge, I'll throw you off it!
30 My uncle's options were suddenly limited. He knew that if he gave the thug the thousand naira, his whole wallet could get

---

2 **limber** agile, fit – 3 **to brook** to allow – 5 **strut** proud walk – 6 **swagger** confident walk – 11 **undiluted**˙ pure – 11 **gait** walk, posture – 13 **unequivocal** [ʌn.ɪ'kwɪv.ə.kᵊl] clear – 19 **to accost** to speak to sb in an aggressive way – 25 **to cave in** to give in – 26 **hostile**˙ aggressive – 31 **thug** criminal

cleaned out. The man could tell him to take off his trousers and crawl on all fours in the dirt or something similarly humiliating. On the other hand, he really did look like the kind of guy who could make good on his threat of murder.

Uncle Bello's instincts told him to fight fire with fire. He had lived in Europe for a long time, studying management in Krakow in the 1980s. In fact he was still fluent in Polish. But he had also grown up in a relatively poor family, and had had to fend for himself from an early age. So he knew the ways of the street. He started shouting at the man:

–Waste me? Waste *me*? Are your eyes functioning? Look at me very well before you say another word. You don't recognize me? I will injure you, I will *kill* you. You understand? I will kill you! Do you know who you are talking to? Ehn? Do you know me? I will make your wife a widow!

"But, of course," my uncle added with a deep laugh, "the whole time I was saying this, I was *quaking* in my shoes like you wouldn't believe." The guy bought the act though, and started begging my uncle to forgive him. Finally, my uncle gave him another two hundred, and they parted ways. About three dollars had changed hands. Both lived to tell the tale. Lagos.

As I make my way through the crowd at Ojodu–Berger, a cellphone and a small digital camera are in the front pockets of my jeans. My shoulders are dropped back, my face is tensed, my eyes narrowed. It is difficult to keep from overdoing it at first, hard to recall how I had managed all those years ago, but I soon find the right register. The trick is to present an outward attitude of alertness, while keeping a calm and observant mood within. And there also has to be the will to be violent, a will that has to be available when it is called for. I am determined not to crawl on all fours or bark like a dog. I am especially conscious that my light complexion could make me a target out here.

17 **to quake** to shake – 26 **to recall** to remember – 27 **register** *here:* way, style –
28 **alertness** watchfulness – 32 **complexion** skin color

I easily locate one of the buses plying the Obalende–CMS route. It is neither more nor less rickety than any of the others. They are all in bad shape, but they are all functional. I climb in, squeezed between two men in the back row. One of the men
5 wears a sky-blue baseball cap and has a swollen eye. The other man is older. He reads a newspaper. The bus fills quickly and we all begin to sweat. Someone pushes a window open and a cooling breeze curls around the bus. That is when I see her.

1 **to ply** to work, to do – 2 **rickety** wobbly, unstable

EIGHT

The penultimate passenger to enter the danfo at Ojodu–Berger
is a woman in an *adire* blouse. She holds a large book. The book's
dust jacket is off-white, matte. I cannot see her face, though I
try to. But, as she sits down, I crane my neck to see what is
5 printed on the book cover, and I catch sight of the author's name.
What I see makes my heart leap up into my mouth and thrash
about like a catfish in a bucket: Michael Ondaatje. It was he who
had the dream about acrobats in a great house. Now to find a
reader of Ondaatje in these circumstances. It is incongruous,
10 and I could hardly be more surprised had she started singing a
tune from *Des Knaben Wunderhorn*.

Of course, Nigerians read. There are the readers of newspapers,
such as the gentleman next to me. Magazines of various kinds
are popular, as are religious books. But an adult reading a
15 challenging work of literary fiction on Lagos public transportation: that's a sight rare as hen's teeth. The Nigerian literacy rate
is low, estimated at fifty-seven percent. But, worse, actual literary habits are inculcated in very few of the so-called literate. I
meet only a small number of readers, and those few read
20 tabloids, romance novels by Mills & Boon, or tracts that promise
"victorious living" according to certain spiritual principles. It is
a hostile environment for the life of the mind. Once we pass the
overpass at Ojota, the rush-hour congestion eases. The speed
we are gathering on the road means the journey is surprisingly
25 cool. The breeze through the open window is constant. The man
next to me folds away his newspaper and begins to nod. Everyone else stares into space. The reader, of whom I can see only
scarf and shoulders, reads.

---

1 **penultimate** last but one – 2 **adire** indigo-dyed cloth made in southwestern Nigeria
by Yoruba women – 6 **to thrash** to beat – 7 **Michael Ondaatje** (* 1943) Canadian author
of Sri Lankan origin ("The English Patient") – 11 **Des Knaben Wunderhorn** collection of
German folk songs by Clemens Brentano und Achim von Arnim (1805) – 16 **literacy**˚
reading ability – 18 **to inculcate** to train, to infuse

Mysterious woman. The condition of the book, from the brief glimpse I have of it, suggests that it is new. Where could she have bought it? Only in two or three of the few bookshops I know of in the city. And if she bought it in Lagos, how much
5 would it have cost her? More than any normal rider of the Lagos public transportation would consider reasonable, that much is certain. Why, then, is she on the bus? Because it is what she could afford, or is it because she, too, is an eccentric? The questions come to my mind one after the other, and I cannot
10 untangle them. I hunger for conversation with my secret sharer, about whom, because I know this one thing, I know many things.

–What, lady, do you make of Ondaatje's labyrinthine sentences, his sensuous prose? How does his intense visuality strike you? But is it hard to concentrate on such poetry in Lagos traffic, with
15 the noise of the crowd, and the tout's body odor wafting over you? I see all those gathered here, and I believe in you most.

My mind runs a monologue as I watch the back of her head for the duration of the journey. I hope that she will not get off the bus before my stop at CMS, so that I can hop off as she does,
20 walk alongside her, interrogate her. So that I can say to her, with the wild look common to all those who are crazed by overidentification, "We must talk. We have much to say to each other. Let me explain." In the last row of the danfo, I work on my courage. Lagosians are distrustful of strangers, and I have
25 to speak the right words to win her confidence. The bus crosses from Yaba over the Third Mainland Bridge into Lagos Island. In the shadow of skyscrapers, half-nude men in dugouts cast nets into the lagoon. The work of arms and shoulders. I think of Auden's line: Poetry makes nothing happen. The bus comes to
30 a stop. She disembarks, at Obalende, with her book, and quickly

13 **sensuous** *here:* rich, appealing to the senses – 15 **to waft** to drift – 27 **dugout** trench, shelter – 29 **Auden's line: Poetry makes nothing happen** quote from the poem "In Memory of W.B Yeats" by W. H. Auden (1907–1973)

vanishes into the bookless crowd. Just like that, she is gone. Gone, but seared into my mind still. That woman, evanescent as an image made with the lens wide open.

2 **seared** burnt – 2 **evanescent** passing

NINE

There is seating for up to thirty under the white canopy. The program is well under way when one of the last guests finally arrives. She is an ample woman with a regal presence. She is ushered to a seat near the high table, breaking into smiles as
5 she catches my aunt's eye. My cousins and I are seated several rows behind. I don't recognize her.

–Oh, that's Mrs. Adelaja.

Mrs. Adelaja? It only gradually becomes clear to me who she is. I have never met her but I know her by reputation: she was
10 a colleague to Aunty Folake for many years. They had worked in the same government ministry, and not long after I left, Mrs. Adelaja had become quite a close friend of the family. Muyiwa says:

–She lost her husband.

15 –Oh, yes, that I think I heard about. How sad.

–Yes, but the really sad thing is the way it happened.

The rhetoric and rites of the engagement introduction continue around us. Someone in the bride's family, on the other side of the dais, speaks into a microphone about the couple.
20 The bride-to-be, Alaba, is absent. She is a banker in Cape Town. Her groom, my cousins' cousin, Dayo, has come with his family to formally present himself to his future in-laws.

–It was armed robbers, Muyiwa says. It happened in 1998.

The woman's skin glows with warm ocher tones, and her eyes
25 flash intelligently each time she speaks or laughs. I observe her intently from where I sit. She must be about fifty-five.

–The men came into their house at night, an armed gang. Woke up the parents, their children, the house help.

–And they shot him?

---

1 **canopy** cover, tent-like protection – 3 **ample** *here:* big – 4 **to usher** to escort –
19 **dais** platform, podium – 22 **in-laws** family of the bridegroom or bride –
28 **house help** maid

46

–No.

Home invasions were extremely common in Lagos in the 1990s, and they still happen, though less frequently. My own family had two encounters with armed robbers. Once, when I was at Aunty Folake's place on a long vacation, the men had got into the compound but had been unable to break down the reinforced doors leading into the house. We had all huddled in the bathroom of the master bedroom while the robbers threatened from outside. They kept at it, ramming the massive front door repeatedly, until it was almost the break of day. Only then, thwarted, did they give up and melt away with the shadows. We emerged from behind the barricades long after the sun had risen, and saw that one of the robbers must have been injured scaling the broken-glass-topped fence. We found drops on the concrete all the way along the walls surrounding the house and leading to the front door, the blood he'd left behind like ominous petals.

These robbers, or some others like them, came back a few years later. This was after I had left for America. This time, they got in. Uncle Tunde had been punched in the face. Muyiwa, who was about eight at the time, had been slapped. All the electronics, jewelry, and money in the house were taken. For many years afterward, Aunty Folake couldn't sleep through the night. Uncle Tunde bought a gun. It was never fired, not even in practice. It just hung there on the bedroom wall, rusting. It was a mysterious presence in the family home, a Chekhovian prop awaiting its fruition in vain.

–They cleaned out the house, but when they were leaving, they forced Mr. Adelaja to come with them.

The master of ceremonies makes a wisecrack that has both the bride's and the groom's families convulsed with laughter.

---

6 **reinforced**˚ [ˌriːɪnˈfɔrst] secure, made stronger – 7 **huddled** crowded together – 11 **thwarted** frustrated – 13 **to scale** to climb – 16 **petal** part of a flower – 26 **fruition** fulfilment – 29 **wisecrack** joke – 30 **convulsed** shaking

The bride's family has selected a peach-colored theme for the occasion, and all their headwear is of the same fabric. At the laughter, Muyiwa and I both look up, then look down again, and Muyiwa continues his story.

5 –They locked him up in the trunk of his car, and drove around to the neighbor's house. When they got there, they dragged him out and made him speak into the intercom. "It's your neighbor. Please. I need some help. Please open the gate." This was at two in the morning. Mr. Adelaja was the kind of man you opened
10 your gate to, at any time of day. A respectable man, well known in the neighborhood, well liked. And that way, the robbers gained access to the neighbor's place, cleaned out *his* house. Then, they dragged him along too, left his wife and daughters weeping and pleading. So now, there are two men in the trunk of the car, and
15 they can hear the armed robbers discussing their strategy. They can hear them saying, Well, these guys have seen our faces and heard our voices. We're going to have to kill them. And then they come round, and they open the trunk, and they shoot Mr. Adelaja twice, once in the stomach and once in the head. The neighbor,
20 they leave alive, hoping to use him as bait for some more houses. They shut the trunk. But not long after that, they run into a police checkpoint. Panicked, they jump out of the car and disappear into the woods. And the police examine the car, and in the trunk they find two men, both covered in blood, one man
25 still alive.

Muyiwa shakes his head. I look at Mrs. Adelaja again, this woman in whose radiance I can see nothing that looks like grief and nothing that looks like the terrible humiliation in the story. But this is what those bastards have saddled her with for the
30 rest of her life: the memory of the man she loves forever tied to the degradation of that one night. I muse on how they would have gone to bed that evening like any other aging married

7 **intercom** *Sprechanlage* – 20 **bait** *Köder* – 27 **radiance** happiness, beauty

couple, perhaps with tender words, or perhaps in the midst of some minor tiff, with no thought of the violence that would soon tear them from each other. I imagine her in the weeks and months afterward, her beautiful face disfigured by sorrow. And
5 then the gradual courage to continue, the strength she had to find for herself and for her children. Fortitude beyond imagining. It is a great and painful wonder to me, just at that moment, that there is no trace of it on her face, no visible mark, seven years on.

10 Under the white canopy, the bride's family has begun to serve soft drinks and *jollof* rice and *moin-moin*. I look around at the groom's family, my family. The men wear purple *aso oke* caps, the women shiny purple *geles*. My family, all of whose lives time has altered inexorably. Each face on which my eye rests brings
15 me up short. I see Aunty Arinola, Uncle Tunde's older sister, whose husband collapsed at a market in Benin City, his corpse ignored by the public for hours. Two seats from her is the jovial friend of the family, Mr. Hassan. He is my cousin Adebola's godfather; his wife of twenty-seven years was killed in a car crash
20 last year. And I consider myself, consider my own loss, too. Father's memory has already become so insubstantial, fixed to a few events only: a birthday party, a day at the beach, a discussion one evening in the kitchen while I cleaned a fish and he sat at the dining table looking over some notes from work. I
25 cannot even remember what we talked about that night. All I have is the memory of sawing away at the gills while he looked up intermittently from the stack of reports in front of him and talked to me. Sometimes I try to make a mental image of his face at that table on that night, and I fail. I still have photographs,
30 but I no longer know what my father looked like.

---

2 **tiff** argument – 6 **fortitude** strength – 11 **jollof rice** spicy African rice dish – 11 **moin-moin** Nigerian steamed bean pudding – 12 ***aso oke* cap** a type of soft fez, a traditional Yoruba hat – 13 **gele** West-African headdress – 14 **inexorable** inevitable – 21 **insubstantial** weak, unimportant – 26 **gills** *Kiemen* – 27 **intermittently** sporadically

The air under the canopy is full of the aroma of food. We pass plates of rice and chicken down until everybody has one. The invisible past, on this day of celebration, as on every day:

And there, behind it, marched so long a file
5   *Of people, I would never have believed*
That death could have undone so many souls.

4 quote from the English poet T.S. Eliot's (1888–1965) „The Wasteland" (1922)

TEN

Pastor Olakunle strides up and down the stage. He is all energy. He stops, peers into the camera, holds up his Bible, and breaks into a wide white grin. He breathes heavily into the microphone: God is good. God is *gooood.* Pastor Olakunle is delivering a teaching to the faithful. This is a mighty word that the Lord has laid on his heart, praise the Lord. God doesn't want you to be sick, God doesn't want you to die. If only you would believe. You. Shall. Be. Healed, praise the Lord. Our God is not a poor God, nor is he wretched. His true followers can be neither poor nor wretched.

Pastor Olakunle is attired in a silk suit. His shoes are of fine Italian leather, his accent is American, as befits a prosperous man, praise the Lord. Pastor Olakunle is intoxicated with the joy of the Lord. He jumps up and down. One more thing, he says, and this is wonderful: once you are walking in faith, you shall never be sick again. Yes, you heard it right. The Lord will banish all sickness from your life. Healing is yours, in the mighty name of Jesus.

Pastor Olakunle owns several Mercedes-Benz cars. It is not clear if he is living as victoriously as Pastor Michael, who, as is well known, owns both a Rolls-Royce and a Learjet, praise the Lord. But who also, inexplicably, has just died. The Lord moves in mysterious ways. Nevertheless, our God is not a poor God, and Pastor Olakunle does very well. The Church of the New Generation is filled to the rafters, praise the Lord, and when he gives the word about permanent healing, a woman in the audience raises her hand in awe and adoration of the mighty name, rises to her feet, swoons.

---

9 **wretched** ['retʃ.ɪd] unpleasant, bad – 11 **attired** clothed – 12 **prosperous**˙ rich, wealthy – 13 **intoxicated**˙ high, drunk – 25 **rafters** wooden beams supporting a roof – 28 **to swoon** to faint

ELEVEN

Adebola, Muyiwa's brother, had just been born when I left home. Now he is in Class Two of the senior secondary school, thinking about going to university in a year or two. He is a bright boy, ranked in the top twenty in a class of over 250. He is thoughtful
5 and good-natured, and attends Mayflower School in Ikenne, Ogun State. Mayflower, one of Nigeria's most reputable boarding schools, was founded by Tai Solarin in 1956. Solarin was a maverick, much persecuted by the successive military juntas that misruled the country. He died in 1994, and many Nigerians
10 continue to hold him in highest esteem. One reason for this is that, for most of his life, he led the campaign to make elementary education free and compulsory in Nigeria.

   –Tai Solarin was a humanist, Adebola says.

   –That's right, I reply. And do you know what a humanist is?
15 –Yes, of course. A humanist is someone who doesn't believe in God.

   –Oh no, Adebola. That's not the definition of a humanist.

   –Tai Solarin is a humanist. And Tai Solarin doesn't believe in God.
20 –Both of those things are true. But neither follows from the other. A humanist is someone who believes in humanity, someone who celebrates human ability and potential. That's where we get the word "humanities" from. A person who doesn't believe in God is an atheist.
25 –A humanist is someone who doesn't believe in God. That's what we were told at school.

---

7 **Tai Solarin** (1922 – 1994) Author and educator. He founded the famous Mayflower School. He was also one of the post-Independence civil rights critics and activists in his native Nigeria – 8 **maverick** nonconformist, unusual person – 10 **to hold sb in high esteem** ˟ to highly respect sb – 12 **compulsory** ˟ obligatory

TWELVE

One goes to the market to participate in the world. As with all things that concern the world, being in the market requires caution. The market–as the essence of the city–is always alive with possibility and danger. Strangers encounter each other in the world's infinite variety; vigilance is needed. Everyone is there not merely to buy or sell, but because it is a duty. If you sit in your house, if you refuse to go to market, how would you know of the existence of others? How would you know of your own existence?

When I start speaking Yoruba, the man I've been haggling with over some carved masks laughs nervously. "Ah *oga*," he says, "I didn't know you knew the language, I took you for an *oyinbo*, or an Ibo man!" I'm irritated. What subtle tells of dress or body language have, again, given me away? This kind of thing didn't happen when I lived here, when I used to pass through this very market on my way to my exam preparation lessons.

The Tejuosho bus stop, a stone's throw from where I stand, is a tangle of traffic, mostly danfos and molues, that one might be tempted to describe as one of the densest spots of human activity in the city, were the description not also true of many other neighborhoods: Ojuelegba, Ikeja, Oshodi, Isolo, Ketu, Ojota.

"Well now that you know I'm not a visitor, you will agree to give me a good price, *abi*?" He shakes his head, searches for excuses. "*Oga*, times are hard, I am not charging you high." He still suspects me of carrying more money than I know what to do with. The masks are beautiful, but the price he is asking is exorbitant. I leave his shop and move on. Other vendors call me. "*Oga*, boss, look my side now, I go give una good price." Others simply call out: "*Oyinbo*." "White man." Young men sit

---

5 **vigilance**• watchfulness, caution – 10 **to haggle** to barter *(handeln)* – 11 **oga** *inf.* Pidgin English: man, dude

in the interiors of the small stalls on raffia mats or on low stools, their limbs unfurled. They are passing time, waiting for the next thing, in bodies designed for activity far more vigorous than this. I move through the warren of shops, which, like a souk, is cool and overstuffed, delighting in its own tacky variety, spilling seamlessly into the cavernous indoor shop. Piles of bright plastic buckets line the entrance, and beyond them, the cloth merchants–these ones are women, *alhajas*–swaddled in laces and looking out with listless gazes. The hall is not well lit. It is as if the outdoor market is reclaiming for itself what had been designed to be a mall. It was my favorite of all the markets, because of this interior coolness. The only movement here is from the stream of customers, and the slow surveillance of the standing fans. The concrete underfoot is curiously soft, tempered with use. Then I emerge to sunlight and the sudden hysteria of car horns and engines. Six roads meet here and there are no traffic lights. Congestion is the rule, to which there is rarely exception. Here, I'm told, is where the boy was killed.

He was eleven years old. He snatched a bag from inside the market, six weeks ago. I know the rest, even before I'm told: I've seen it before. At least, I've seen it in its constituent parts, if never all at once. I watched in fragments and was unimpressed, as children are by whatever seems to them to be normal. I was still a child when I learned to stitch the various vignettes into a single story. The desperate grab, the cries of thief–an ordinary cry anywhere else, but in a Lagos market, it thins the blood out with fear–the cry taken up by those who never saw the original theft, but who nevertheless believe in its motivating power. It was like this the day I was at the *garri* stall with my mother. I could have been no more than seven. Cries of thief, thief. Then

---

1 **raffia** straw – 2 **unfurled** spread out – 3 **vigorous**° strong, energetic – 4 **warren** labyrinth – 4 **souk** bazaar – 5 **tacky** cheap, low quality – 6 **seamlessly** without distinction, unnoticably – 6 **cavernous** large open space inside – 8 **swaddled** wrapped – 14 **tempered** hardened – 21 **constituent** *here:* individual – 24 **vignette** piece – 29 **garri** flour-like foodstuff

the chase that arises organically and with frightening swiftness out of the placid texture of the market, a furious wave of men that organizes itself into a single living thing. And then the capture of the felon–there is nowhere to run–his denials and,
5 when those inevitably fail, his pleas. He's never far into the pleas before he is pushed–all this I've seen, more than once–kicked, beaten with what never looks like less than a personal aggravation by other men whom he has never met. The violence is intimate, interspersed with curses. The stolen bag has, by now,
10 made its way back into the hands of the madame, and she has cleared out of the scene. If nothing was stolen, nothing is returned, but the event must always run its course.

Someone pushes me out of the way. I am daydreaming at the market, making myself a target. This is pure idiocy. I check my
15 pockets, make sure I still have my wallet on me, and push my way into the crowd that has gathered in the intersection. Traffic is stalled. I have come for this, to see with my own eyes where this thing happened.

The boy is eleven, but he has eaten poorly all his life and looks
20 much younger. He is crying. He is trying to explain something. Someone told me to do it, he says, that man over there. He points. It's futile. A wiry man steps forward and slaps him hard. It's not a bag, it turns out; it's a baby he's accused of stealing. Everyone knows that you can use a stolen baby to make money,
25 to literally manufacture cash, in alliance with unseen occult powers. An old car tire–from where?–has been quickly sourced. The boy's clothes are torn off, he is knocked down repeatedly. Space has been created out of the congestion. A gaggle of schoolgirls, in green-and-white uniforms, has joined the
30 spectators. And a new twist: in the crowd, there stands a man

---

2 **placid** ['plæs.ɪd] easy-going, calm – 4 **felon**˙ criminal – 8 **aggravation** annoyance, trouble – 9 **interspersed** sprinkled – 16 **intersection**˙ crossing – 17 **stalled** stopped – 22 **futile**˙ pointless – 22 **wiry** thin and tough *(drahtig)* – 28 **gaggle** group

with a digital camcorder. The single eye of his machine collects the event: this fragile body, which, shed of clothes, is now like a dark sapling whipped about in the wind. The tire is flung around the boy. He is losing consciousness but revives with
5 sudden panic when he is doused with petrol. From the distance, two traffic officers, the ones they call Yellow Fever, watch. The splashing liquid is lighter than water, it is fragrant, it drips off him, beads in his woolly hair. He glistens. The begging stops. He stops begging and he is not yet lit. The whites of his eyes are
10 bright as lamps. And then only the last thing, which is soon supplied. The fire catches with a loud gust, and the crowd gasps and inches back. The boy dances furiously but, hemmed down by the tire, quickly goes prone, and still. The most vivid moment in the fire's life passes, and its color dulls and fizzes out. The
15 crowd, chattering and sighing, momentarily sated, melts away. The man with the digicam lowers his machine. He, too, disappears. Traffic quickly reconstitutes around the charred pile. The air smells of rubber, meat, and exhaust.

In a few days, it will be as though nothing happened. There
20 are those who will copy the tape, it will move around, perhaps provide some grim entertainment for the men in the shops, or in police stations, or homes. It will finally be broadcast on the national news, to outrage, and to an instant forgetting. I cannot find the will to hunt the tape down, but I hear about it here and
25 there. A wick, nameless, snuffed. And what if he was only eleven? A thief is a thief; his master will find another boy, another one without a name. The market has seen everything. It must eat. It does not break its habits.

---

2 **shed** without, removed – 3 **sapling** seedling *(Spross)* – 5 **to douse** to soak – 8 **to glisten**˙ [ˈglɪsᵊn] to shine, to gleam – 11 **gust**˙ breeze – 12 **to inch back** to slowly move back *(zurückweichen)* – 13 **to go prone** to lie down – 15 **sated** satisfied – 17 **charred**˙ burnt – 25 **wick**˙ part of a candle that burns *(Docht)* – 25 **to snuff** to put out

For my part, I need to find the danfo that goes from here to Yaba. It only takes a moment. The conductor's song draws me, to the other side of the pedestrian bridge. The vehicle is newer than most. It has a sticker on its back window: "God's Time Is
5   the Best Time." And under that another one: "He's a Fine Guy." I enter the bus and leave the scene.

THIRTEEN

The air in the strange, familiar environment of this city is dense
with story, and it draws me into thinking of life as stories. The
narratives fly at me from all directions. Everyone who walks into
the house, every stranger I engage in conversation, has a
5   fascinating story to deliver. The details I find so alluring in Gabriel
García Márquez are here, awaiting their recording angel. All I
have to do is prod gently, and people open up. And that literary
texture, of lives full of unpredictable narrative, is what appeals.
There is a romantic aspect to this. I think of Vikram Seth, who
10 abandoned his doctoral studies at Stanford and moved to India
to write *A Suitable Boy*. The monk-like solitude in his room at
home, the meals prepared and then announced with a discreet
knock on his door. Or the example of García Márquez, when he
was writing *One Hundred Years of Solitude*. Complete devotion
15 to the task, the unwavering support of a partner, and a confidence
in his own gifts, a confidence he knows the public will come to
share. The ghosts of his early failures are not allowed to interfere
with this vision.
One morning, walking outside the estate to where the Isheri
20 Road joins the Lagos–Sagamu Expressway Bridge, I witness a
collision between two cars. Immediately, both drivers shut off
their engines, jump out of their vehicles, and start beating each
other up. They fight fiercely but without malice, as if this is an
ancient ritual they both have to undergo, less for the right-of-
25 way than to prove their manliness. When someone from the
gathering crowd eventually pulls them apart, I see that one of
the men is bleeding at the mouth.

---

5 **alluring** attractive, interesting – 5 **Gabriel García Márquez** (1927–2014) Columbian
author, best known for *One Hundred Years of Solitude* – 7 **to prod** to push, to persuade –
9 **Vikram Seth** (*1952) Indian novelist and poet – 15 **unwavering** firm – 23 **malice**•
wickedness, hatred

Well, this is wonderful, I think. Life hangs out here. The pungent details are all around me. It is a paradise for the lover of gossip. Just one week later, I see another fight, at the very same bend in the road. All the touts in the vicinity join in this one. It is pandemonium, but a completely normal kind, and it fizzles out after about ten minutes. End of brawl. Everyone goes back to his normal business. It is an appalling way to conduct a society, yes, but I suddenly feel a vague pity for all those writers who have to ply their trade from sleepy American suburbs, writing divorce scenes symbolized by the very slow washing of dishes. Had John Updike been African, he would have won the Nobel Prize twenty years ago. I feel sure that his material hobbled him. Shillington, Pennsylvania, simply did not measure up to his extravagant gifts. And sadder yet are those who haven't even a fraction of Updike's talent and yet must hoe the same arid patch for stories. No such aridity here, but that doesn't mean I can just move to Nigeria. There are practical issues to consider. There is the question of money, the question of my professional development and my other work. Serious questions for which there are answers. But there is also the question of my tolerance for the environment. Am I ready for all the rage Nigeria can bring out of me? The various run-ins a "humanist" might have in such a place as this? My first few nights in Lagos, I actually enjoy the power cuts. Muyiwa and I take bets about whether electricity will see us past 10:00 P.M. on a given night. It rarely does. The television flickers into nothingness, the room is instantly swallowed up by shadow, and the ceiling fans whir to a stop. Depending on how late it is, we might switch on the generator or we might leave it off. Rarely do we have the generator going right through the night.

2 **pungent** sharp – 5 **pandemonium** chaos – 6 **brawl**° fight – 11 **John Updike** (1932 – 2009) American novelist who won the Pulitzer Prize three times – 12 **to hobble** *here:* to hinder – 15 **to hoe**° to dig *(umgraben, beackern)* – 15 **arid**° dry

Power comes back at 4:00 A.M. or later. The fan resumes its spinning like a broken conversation continued in midsentence. Lightbulbs hiss back to brightness in the hallway and living room. The heat is difficult to deal with at night, and often I don't
5 get to sleep until the power is restored. Only then, as the fan cools the room down, do I finally fade out of consciousness. But within an hour or two the sun comes up, the muezzin and the cockerels begin their daily contest, and any further hope of sleep is futile. The hardest thing to deal with, after weeks of constant
10 power cuts, is the noise of the generators. The house, which was quite large to begin with, has been carved up into three sizable apartments. Two have been rented out to other families, an arrangement that supplements my relatives' income. One negative result of this arrangement is that there are now three
15 loud diesel generators in the compound. When they all come on, as they do nightly, I can feel my mind fraying. I don't experience the real privilege that it is for these three families to have the generators in a city where so many sit in darkness. The noise, the dark gray plumes of the diesel smoke are foremost in
20 my mind: the moment there is a power cut, my evening is finished. The neighbors downstairs watch South African sitcoms at top volume. My bedroom, near the generator house, is filled with the din. It is impossible to hear myself think. I would prefer, on these evenings, to sit in silence with a candle, but that is not
25 a decision I can make for the eighteen other individuals in the compound.

This is but one issue out of many. Combined with traffic congestion, which is a serious problem in Lagos, and considering the thousand natural shocks to which the average Nigerian is
30 subject–the police, the armed robbers, the public officials, the government, the total absence of social services, the poor distribution of amenities–the environment is anything but

16 **to fray** to wear out – 19 **plume** cloud-like – 23 **din** noise – 32 **amenity** *(usu Pl)* [ə'men.ə.ti] sth that provides comfort and pleasure or is thought necessary to live comfortably (e.g. hot water)

tranquil. I have newfound respect for anyone who accomplishes any kind of creative work in the country. Like the Nigerian photographers I met at an event at the Goethe-Institut: people who, against all odds, keep an artistic struggle alive. I admire
5 them anew.

There is a disconnect between the wealth of stories available here and the rarity of creative refuge. There is no computer at the house, but I had hoped at least to sit quietly in the bedroom in the evenings and do some writing. It proves difficult to do so.
10 Not in daylight, with all the running around to do and people to see, and not at night, with the smell of diesel lacing the air, and the wail of a trio of power-generating engines mixing with the loud singing from the churches in the middle distance. Writing is difficult, reading impossible. People are so exhausted
15 after all the hassle of a normal Lagos day that, for the vast majority, mindless entertainment is preferable to any other kind. This is the secret price paid for all those cumulative stresses of Lagos life: the ten-minute journeys that take forty-five minutes, the rarity of places of refuge, the constant confrontation with
20 needs more abject than your own. By day's end, the mind is worn, the body ragged. The best I can manage is to take a few photographs. For the rest of the month, I neither read nor write.

And yet, and yet. The place exerts an elemental pull on me. There is no end of fascinations. People talk all the time, calling
25 on a sense of reality that is not identical to mine. They have wonderful solutions to some nasty problems; in this I see a nobility of spirit that is rare in the world. But also, there is much sorrow, not only of the dramatic kind but also in the way that difficult economic circumstances wear people down, eroding
30 them, preying on their weaknesses, until they do things that

3 **Goethe-Institut** German culture institute – 4 **against all odds** * *gegen alle Erwartungen* – 12 **wail** whine – 20 **abject** extreme – 21 **ragged** worn out – 23 **to exert** to use *(ausüben)* – 30 **to prey on one's weakness** to make sb even weaker

they themselves find hateful, until they are shadows of their best selves. The problem used to only be the leadership. But now, when you step out into the city, your oppressor is likely to be your fellow citizen, his ethics eroded by years of suffering and life at the cusp of desperation. There is venality in abundance here, and the general air of surrender, of helplessness, is the most heartbreaking thing about it. I decide that I love my own tranquillity too much to muck about in other people's troubles. I am not going to move back to Lagos. No way. I don't care if there are a million untold stories, I don't care if that, too, is a contribution to the atmosphere of surrender.

I am going to move back to Lagos. I must. I lie in bed, on my back, wearing only boxer shorts, enduring the late afternoon's damp heat. I have headphones on, and I am listening to "Giant Steps," that twisting, modal argument of saxophone, drums, bass, and piano that is like a repeated unmaking and remaking of the audible world. It is at high volume, but the generators say, No, you will not enjoy this. I have no right to Coltrane here, not with everything else going on. This is Lagos. I disagree, turn the volume up, listen to both the music and the noise. Neither gives way. No sense emerges of the combat between art and messy reality.

5 **cusp** point – 5 **venality** act of being bought or obtained for money *(Bestechlichkeit)* – 14 **"Giant Steps"** jazz song by John Coltrane

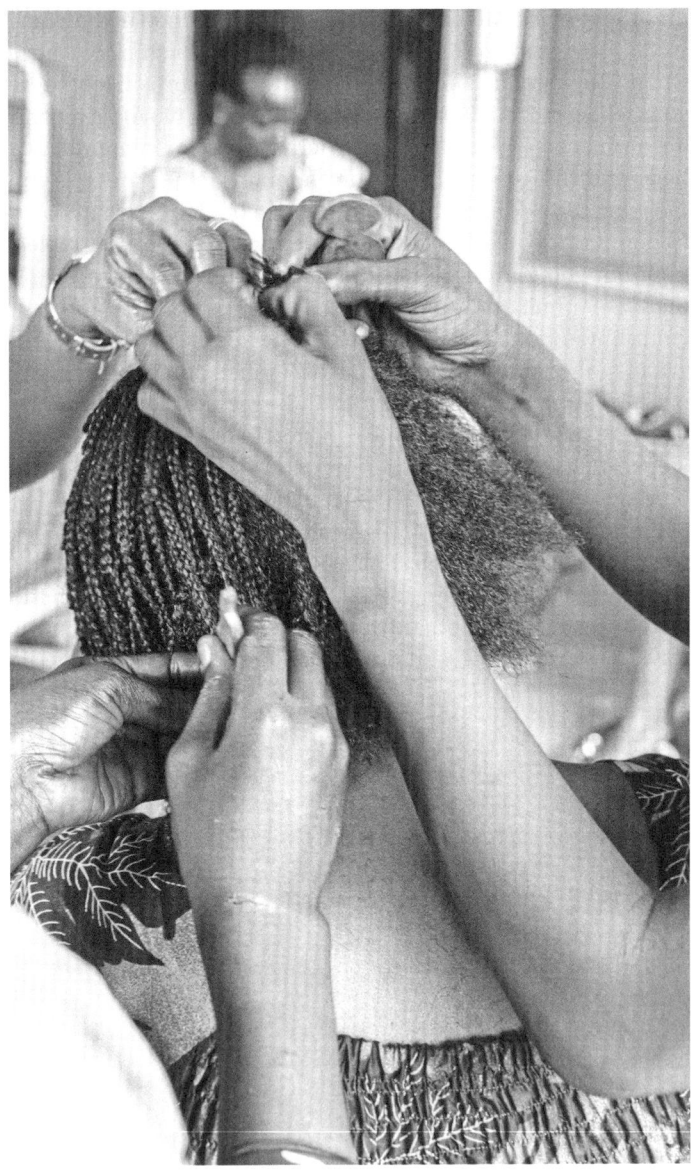

FOURTEEN

The National Museum is in Onikan in the heart of old Lagos.
This part of the city has much in common with other faded
colonial centers. The legacy of foreign rule is visible in the
churches, the Brazilian-style buildings, the porticoed and
decrepit institutions that lace the tiny, winding streets. Alongside
these are the gleaming modern buildings that announce Lagos
Island as the national center of commerce. It is the same thing
one might observe in Bombay around Victoria Terminus, a
combination of the borrowed old and the uncertain new. The
museum sits in a less choked section of Onikan, in the shadow
of the Tafawa Balewa Square stadium, across the street from the
vibrant headquarters of the Musical Society of Nigeria, next to
the brand-new Doric-porticoed City Mall.

The museum has no share in the glamour of these buildings.
It consists of three or four low buildings set at the end of a drive
fringed with manicured lawns. On the morning of my visit, the
grounds are quiet. A sweeper is at his calm work. Behind the
blue ironwork grille at the entrance is a pair of giant pots. The
reception window, which opens into the vestibule, has a sign
announcing an entry fee of fifty naira. The listless woman at the
reception sends me to the ticket office, which is five yards away
from where she sits. I buy a ticket from another woman and, as
neither the receptionist nor the ticket agent looks keen to answer
questions, walk into the first of the galleries. There are no
brochures available about the collection. There are no books or
prints for sale. There is no gift shop.

I have looked forward to this visit for many years because the
National Museum has been a memorial touchstone for me.
During my years in the United States and in Europe, many of

---

2 **faded**˙ pale, washed-out – 3 **legacy**˙ [ˈleg.ə.si] heritage – 4 **porticoed** built with a
covered entrance which is supported by columns – 5 **to lace** to decorate (esp. at the
edges) – 10 **choked** here: crowded – 18 **grille** metal frame, grid

my musings about Nigerian cultural patrimony returned me
mentally to Onikan, to the insubstantial recollection I had of a
place I had last visited as a young schoolboy. All people who are
far from home have something they hold on to. For me, it was
5 the museum and the meaning I had invested in its collection.
   I am the only guest in each of the interlinked galleries I enter.
The rooms are indeed silent, save for the chattering of two
museum staff in one room, and the solitary singing by another
in the next room. The woman sits in a corner and sings from a
10 hymnal as if, for all the world, she were not at a place of work.
She ignores me until, standing at the end of a long row of cases,
I take out my camera and capture an image.
   –Is not allowed!
   –Excuse me?
15 –Is not allowed. Forbidden. No photo.
   She points at the offending contraption, flaps a hand at it,
and fixes me with a withering stare. Her tone is acidic. But the
voice changes back immediately as she picks up the verse
where she left off and resumes sweetly singing the glories of her
20 Lord. Her disconnection from the environment is absolute. A
victorious Christian among the idols. Her voice floats through
the rooms. The galleries, cramped, are spatially unlike what I
remember or had imagined, and the artifacts are caked in dust
and under dirty plastic screens. The whole place has a tired,
25 improvised air about it, like a secondary school assignment
finished years ago and never touched since. The deepest
disappointment, though, is not in presentation. It is in content.
I honestly expected to find the glory of Nigerian archaeology
and art history on display here. I had hoped to see the best of

---

1 **musing** reflection – 1 **patrimony** *here:* heritage – 10 **hymnal** book of prayers and
church songs *(Gesangbuch)* – 16 **contraption** apparatus – 17 **withering** severe, very
critical – 17 **acidic*** [əˈsɪd.ɪk] sharp, unfriendly – 22 **spatially** relating to space and the
relationship of objects within it – 23 **artifact** piece of art

the Ife bronzes, the fine Benin brass plaques and figures, Nok terra-cotta, the roped vessels of Igbo-Ukwu, the art for which Nigeria is justly admired in academies and museums the world over.

5　　It is not to be. Though there are examples of each kind of art, they are few, are rarely of the best quality, and are meagerly documented. The whole enterprise is clotted with a weird reticence. It is clear that no one cares about the artifacts. There are such gaps in the collection that one can only imagine that
10　there has been recent plunder. The best pieces have probably found their way into the hands of dealers in Paris, Zurich, and elsewhere. My recent experience of Nigerian art at the Metropolitan Museum in New York was excellent. The same had been true at the British Museum, as well as at the Museum für
15　Völkerkunde in Berlin. A clean environment, careful lighting, and, above all, outstanding documentation that set the works in the proper cultural context. What each of those places had done was create a desire in me to see this astonishing art at its best, to see it in its own home. London, New York, and Berlin
20　had made me long for Lagos. The West had sharpened my appetite for ancient African art. And Lagos is proving a crushing disappointment.

I am aware of the troubled history of the collecting of African art, the way colonial authorities had carted off treasures to their
25　capitals in the nineteenth and early twentieth centuries. But I also know how rich Nigerian museums had been as recently as the 1960s and '70s, when the British archaeologists Frank Wilson and John Wallace had been curators here. Wilson is an authority

---

1 **Ife** (Yoruba: Ifè, also Ilé-Ifè) an ancient Yoruba city in south-western Nigeria – 1 **Benin**, also known as the **Benin** Kingdom, is a pre-colonial kingdom in what is now southern Nigeria – 1 **Nok** culture is an early Iron Age population of northern Nigeria, famous for their terracotta sculptures which were first discovered in 1928 – 2 archaeology of **Igbo-Ukwu** revealed bronze artifacts from the 9th century A.D. – 8 **reticence**˚ restraint (Zurückhaltung) – 10 **plunder**˚ stealing (Plünderung)

on Ife art, and Wallace a fine ethnographer of Yoruba and Riverine art. And after them there was the outstanding art historian Udoh Udoh, who was director of the National Museum. These men are academics, and they were careful to document and present
5 what was entrusted to them. But, as with many other national institutions during the military years, in the 1980s the museums likely became sinecures for whoever got posted to them. I remember a conversation I had with Wallace at London's School of Oriental and African Studies in 1999. A gentle, deeply learned
10 man, he had gone to Nigeria with the British Colonial Service and risen to the top of the old Department of Art and Antiquities. He told me that one of the directors of the Lagos museum had been too superstitious to handle some of the items in his care. The man was a *mallam,* and he feared the fetish power of the
15 masks and statues. According to Wallace, many items simply gathered dust in the basement.

What I see of the place gives me no great reason for thinking that a single thing has been improved in the past twenty years. I step out of the first set of galleries into a small courtyard. Along
20 the walls, there are white cardboard plaques about various Nigerian kingship ceremonies, as well as one about a German-led archaeological expedition in Ijebuland in the 1980s. The print quality is poor, faded from exposure to the sun, and the plaques are badly mildewed. The mildew has eaten into the text
25 and photographs in several places. The cardboard is curled up around the edges. Again, there is the inescapable feeling that one is looking at a neglected high school project. The courtyard itself is sometimes rented out for birthday parties or funerals: a friend had mentioned to me that the party for her grand-

---

1 **Riverine area** of the Niger Delta is a coastal belt of swamps bordering the Atlantic ocean – 7 **sinecure** ['saɪ.nə.kjʊr] job in which someone is paid to do little or no work – 13 **superstitious*** irrational belief in luck and magic *(abergläubisch)* – 14 **mallam** title given to Islamic scholars in Africa – 24 **mildewed*** covered in mold *(schimmelig)*

mother's funeral had been held here. So Nigerians do come to the museum, if only for a weekend party.

I enter the small gallery devoted to the royal art of Benin, and catch sight of a pair of tourists leaving the museum. Their language and bearing make me identify them as foreigners; Brazilians, I think. How sad to travel all the way from Rio or Bahia in pursuit of one's heritage, only to meet with this. The two Brazilians are the only other visitors I see at the museum during the two hours I am there. In the Benin gallery, an employee strides purposefully toward me and asks, with a look of great concern, if I have a ticket. I show him the stub in my hand. He says: I just wanted to be sure. About five minutes later another man, equally agitated, sidles up to me and asks if I have obtained the proper ticket for the gallery. I show him my stub. I see, he says, I just wanted to make sure. I can't quite figure out if either man is asking for a bribe. I'm happy to be in the dark over that question.

And that is it; no more galleries. The archaeological collection is pitiful–a few masks, a few beaded baskets, a clutch of figurines. Hardly anything to set the heart racing. Certainly nothing like the magnificent Plexiglas case full of exquisite Ife bronze heads that I had hoped to find. Later on, I read the curious tale of the loss of one particular Benin bronze. In 1973, the then head of state, General Gowon, had telephoned Udoh Udoh to inform him that he was coming over to the museum to select a piece as a gift for the queen of England. Dr. Udoh, the moment he put the phone down, scrambled to put some of the best pieces away into storage and out of harm's way. But how does one hide a whole museum? Gowon arrived in due course, picked a fine Benin queen mother head from the seventeenth century, much to Dr. Udoh's horror, and gave it to Elizabeth II. The queen of England, reasonably enough, assumed it was a replica. She put it on a shelf in the Royal Library. The true status of the piece was not discovered until 2002, when it was brought out for the Jubilee Exhibition. The fact that it was found to be a genuine antique–John Wallace helped detect this–substantially weakened

the Nigerian government's ongoing case for the return of the numerous Benin plaques currently in the British Museum. The strangest thing about that particular Benin queen mother head was that it had originally been plundered by the British in 1897
5 during the "punitive expedition," and only returned in the 1950s to help set up the Nigerian National Museum. It had already crossed the ocean twice before the general, in gratitude for Britain's support of the Federal cause during the Biafran war, gave it away again. And the British, this time around, had no
10 intention of returning the work.

So disoriented am I by the meagerness of the work on offer that I head to the museum's reception desk and, like Oliver Twist, ask if there is any more. Perhaps there's an upper floor I have missed or something like that. The woman looks deeply irritated
15 by the question; I suspect she would be irritated by any question. She points me to the side of the museum, to a building that looks like a shed. The building, bearing an old sign announcing a "temporary exhibition," is an adjunct to the museum, dedicated solely to the history of Nigeria's rulers from the 1914 political
20 amalgamation of the Northern and Southern protectorates to the present day. I think I have had my most dispiriting experience of the day already, but no, there is still more punishment in store for me. The circular shed contains the National Museum's most famous artifact: the bullet-riddled black Mercedes-Benz in which
25 the head of state General Murtala Muhammed was assassinated during the failed coup of February 1976. This car is the only thing most Lagosian schoolchildren remember about the National Museum. Other than the pocked, gleaming vehicle, the display consists only of a series of wall plaques featuring texts

5 **punitive** punishing – 8 **Biafran war** (6 July 1967 – 15 January 1970) war fought between the government of Nigeria and the secessionist state of Biafra – 12 in Charles Dickens' *Oliver Twist*, Oliver asks for more food – 18 **adjunct** addition – 19 **1914 political amalgamation of the Northern and Southern protectorates** the merging of the different parts of the country in order to make governance easier for the colonial rulers – 21 **dispiriting** demoralizing

about Nigerian history and photographs of the main protagonists.
There are no artifacts, and no documents. The plaques, made
of thick card, as in the courtyard, are extremely rudimentary,
and they, too, have succumbed to mildew. The photos depict
5 Lord Lugard, Aminu Kano, Obafemi Awolowo, Nnamdi Azikiwe,
Tafawa Balewa, and others. The first of the historical texts in the
display reads as follows: "In the early part of the nineteenth
century, the efforts of various abolitionists gradually brought
the obnoxious practice of slavery to an end."

10 And that is the depth of it. The Atlantic slave trade, with
hundreds of thousands of our compatriots sold, tortured,
murdered, was an "obnoxious practice." This underwhelming
text was doubtless written by a colonial officer, probably a few
decades ago, but someone else keeps it hanging there, year after
15 year, as an official Nigerian response to slavery. As I read the
plaque devoted to each regime, my spirit sinks further. The
alleged achievements of each military ruler are listed. The
historical record–and again, this is the National Museum–is
sycophantic, inaccurate, uncritical, and desperately outdated,
20 as if each dictator was sent a form to fill in with his "achievements" and it was left at that. I don't know how to make sense
of what I am looking at. It is as though there is the idea that a
national museum is a good thing to have, but no one has the
interest or ability to present it properly. History, which elsewhere

---

3 **rudimentary*** basic – 4 **to succumb*** to give way – 5 **Lord Lugard** served in Nigeria as
high commissioner and governor and governor-general (1900 – 06) – 5 **Aminu Kano**
(1920 – 1983) Muslim politician from Nigeria. In the 1940s he led a socialist movement
in the northern part of the country in opposition to British rule. – 5 **Obafemi Awolowo**
(1909 – 1987) Nigerian socialist, nationalist and statesman who played a key role in
Nigeria's independence movement. – 5 **Nnamdi Azikiwe** (1904 – 1996) Nigerian
statesman, Governor General of Nigeria from 1960 to 1963 and the first President of
Nigeria from 1963 to 1966. – 6 **Tafawa Balewa** (1912 – 1966) Nigerian politician and the
first prime minister of independent Nigeria. – 8 **abolitionist*** [ˌæb.ə'lɪʃ.ᵊn.ɪst] person
who fights for ending sth, in this case slavery – 9 **obnoxious*** [əb'nɑːk.ʃəs] horrible,
vulgar – 19 **sycophantic** flattering

is a bone of contention, has yet to enter the Nigerian public consciousness, at least judging by institutions like the museum.

The narratives on the three most recent regimes, printed on paper, are tacked near the end of the circular gallery. No one could possibly form a positive impression of Nigeria on the basis of this museum. The worst of the butchers that ran the nation aground are celebrated, without exception. Abacha is there, in his dark glasses. Babangida is there, with his grin. The sequence of posters gives an impression of orderliness and continuity in Nigeria's postindependence history, and no analysis of the coups and countercoups that were the rule rather than the exception for changes of regime. What, I wonder, are the social consequences of life in a country that has no use for history? It brings to mind the brusque retort uttered by a character in John Sayles's film *Men with Guns* in response to a tourist's query: "Atrocities? No. No atrocities happened here. That happens in other countries."

When I step out of the shed, the woman at the front desk is slumped over, fast asleep. The time is 1:00 P.M. I walk out of the museum in bad spirits, and I don't really recover until I visit a nearby *buka* for some pounded yam and *egusi* soup.

1 **bone of contention** sth that two people or groups cannot agree about *(Zankapfel)* –
6 **to run sth aground**˙ to damage, to ruin – 7 **Sani Abacha** (1943–1998) Nigerian Army officer and dictator who served as the de facto President of Nigeria from 1993 until his death in 1998 – 8 **Ibrahim Badamasi Babangida** (born 1941), retired Nigerian Army General who was President of Nigeria from 27 August 1985 to 26 August 1993. –
14 **retort**˙reply – 14 **John Sayles's 1997 film** *Men with Guns* story of one man's discovery of what actually happened in the political history of his nation – 16 **atrocity**˙ carnage, murder, act of violence and cruelty – 21 **buka** street food restaurant – 21 **egusi soup** typically contains leaf vegetables, other vegetables, seasonings and meat

FIFTEEN

There could hardly be a stronger contrast to the National Museum than the MUSON Centre, which I visit later on the same afternoon. MUSON was founded in the 1980s and has since that time come to play a leading role in the musical and theatrical life of the country. The grounds of MUSON–the word is an acronym for the Musical Society of Nigeria–are well organized, featuring three main buildings. One houses a world-class auditorium and recital hall, the second is a conservatory, and between the two, set on a pristine lawn, is an upmarket restaurant called La Scala. The creative energies so sorely lacking in the National Museum seem to have been vested here. And clearly, wealthy people are interested in what happens at MUSON. In the parking lot, cars and SUVs gleam in a long, aspirational row: Lexus, BMW, Mercedes-Benz, Audi. Yet the compound is not designed like a fortress, and one has a sense that this is a place for genuine music enthusiasts, that it is not just a playground for the rich and well connected. I have no problems walking right in, though I have no official business to conduct.

Large posters in front of the auditorium announce recent and upcoming shows: a Christmas gala, a choral performance, a fund-raiser for Nigerian breast cancer charities. There is a flyer for a jazz concert featuring the South African trumpeter Hugh Masekela in an appearance with Lagbaja, the most innovative of the current crop of Nigerian musicians. Most fascinating of all is the announcement of a performance of a Molière play by a professional company visiting from France. Culture, at least in this one corner of the city, seems to be alive and well.

The best thing about MUSON is that it is well organized. Better organized, in truth, than I've come to expect anything in

---

10 **sorely** very much – 14 **aspirational** ambitious

Nigeria to be. And yet, it is a largely private venture. Perhaps that is the secret. They know the importance of presentation: the buildings are well maintained. I see several busy gardeners during my visit, patiently potting miniature palms. And MUSON
5 also knows the value of running a nonprofit organization in partnership with corporations: the Agip Recital Hall is named for an oil company, as is the auditorium, Shell Hall. There is also a major sponsorship deal with the business consultancy Accenture.
10 The Nigerian government, that great bungler, is kept out of it. The mere existence of the conservatory surprises me. That it is so well put together is a great pleasure. As I enter the building, it occurs to me that this is an institution that, in terms of setting and infrastructure, could someday rub shoulders with the
15 Juilliard School or the New England Conservatory. I take an irrational pride in the thought. Outside the building, there is a sign that reads: "Muson School of Music. Founded February 13 1989. Provides training in the theory and practice of music." And below that, in smaller letters: "Individual instructions in
20 singing, violin, piano, flute, clarinet, trumpet, cello and classical guitar for all ages. Graded theory and practical examinations conducted in May and November in several centres in Nigeria." This is quite literally music to my ears. Cello lessons, in Lagos. I imagine some gifted child spinning her way through the Bach
25 suites, practicing afternoon after afternoon in the heat, the sound of traffic in the distance, until she has full command of the music's inner spirit, and can bring her hearers into a state of wonder.
    I go up to the reception area, and there meet a plump young
30 man with a pencil mustache. He is seated behind a metal desk, and is talking to a woman when I come in. She is lithe, dark-

1 **venture**• business project – 10 **bungler** incompetent person – 31 **lithe** [laɪð] agile

skinned, and wears glasses. He silently motions me to a seat. Then he gets up from behind his desk and walks slowly, ceremoniously, to the other side of the room, brings out a newspaper from a cabinet, and walks slowly back. He sits down
5   again, opens the newspaper, and, pointing to a column in it, says to the young lady:

–And so, that's what I was talking about. Isn't that interesting?

He hands her the paper, stares into space meaningfully, and eventually, as if he has run out of things to do, turns to me.

10   –How may I be of assistance?

I tell him I was hoping he would be able to answer some of my questions about the conservatory.

–What would you like to know?

–Well, for instance, about the foundation of the school, the
15   courses on offer, costs, standards.

He nods thoughtfully, then gets up again, and waddles across the room to the cabinet. He pulls out a small stack of papers.

–These brochures can fill you in on some details. The school was founded in 1989, and we have grown a lot in the past few
20   years.

–How is the school funded?

–Through school fees and by private donors.

Then he adds, jovially:

–You know, a rich guy like yourself can just give us one million
25   naira. Just like that.

He makes a flicking motion with his hand. I turn to the young lady and ask if she is a student. She says she is a student in the vocal program, a soprano. Her manner is sniffy. I ask what kind of music she specializes in.

30   –Oh, you know, classical and jazz and stuff. I'll be singing in the fund-raiser next week with the MUSON Orchestra.

28 **sniffy** haughty, arrogant

–Who is in the orchestra?

–It's mostly faculty members of the MUSON School.

She has a distracted, birdlike manner. But that's the extent of my conversation with her. She sits there after that, watching us talk. The receptionist says:

–Depending on what you want, you can have either an expatriate or local teacher.

I raise an eyebrow.

–What's the difference?

–Cost. The expatriate teachers cost much more.

I check the fee schedule in the brochure he gave me. What he says is true. It is a sour note. What they are saying is that even a Nigerian teacher who studied at, say, the Peabody Institute or the Royal Academy would be paid at a much lower rate than any white piano teacher.

–But the most important thing, which we emphasize to all incoming students, is that you must own the instrument you wish to learn. We try to be clear about this, but people still act confused. If you want to learn piano, you must have a piano at home. If you want to learn cello, you must own a cello. Flute, trumpet, whatever your instrument is, you must own it.

–Voice?

He chuckles. They have set the bar quite high. Owning a piano, even in the West, is no easy thing. In Nigeria, it is prohibitively expensive for all but the most moneyed. Yet, I can see immediately how complicated it would be to have a rental system in Nigeria, a country in which credit facilities are not well established, and most things, including cars and houses, are still paid for in cash. On the other hand, students could not be compelled to come to the school to practice four or five days a week, the minimum that would be needed to gain proficiency

---

7 **expatriate** sb who doesn't live in their own country, not local – 23 **to set the bar high** to have ambitious expectations *(die Latte hoch anlegen)* – 24 **prohibitively** excessively, very – 30 **to compel** ˙ to force

on an instrument. The transportation situation would make that too burdensome. What this means is that, for now, serious musical instruction in Lagos is available only to the wealthiest and most dedicated Nigerians.

5 Yet, it is better than nothing. As demand and supply both increase, prices will be adjusted. Things will become more egalitarian, the way they already are with private secondary schools. The MUSON School already represents a great leap forward: nothing of this kind was available when I was a high
10 school student. I did not discover my passion for music until I went to America. A younger set of Nigerians might not have to rely on going overseas to develop this area of interest.

The school, and the bold programming of its concert halls, cheers me greatly. To the extent that places like the National
15 Museum kill my desire to live in the country, institutions like the MUSON Centre revive that will. It is important for a people to have something that is theirs, something to be proud of, and for such institutions to have a host of supporters. And it is vital, at the same time, to have a meaningful forum for interacting
20 with the world. So that Molière's work can appear onstage in Lagos, as Soyinka's appears in London. So that what people in one part of the world think of as uniquely theirs takes its rightful place as a part of universal culture.

Art can do that. Literature, music, visual arts, theater, film.
25 The most convincing signs of life I see in Nigeria are connected to the practice of the arts. And it is like this. Each time I am sure that, in returning to Lagos, I have inadvertently wandered into a region of hell, something else emerges to give me hope. A reader, an orchestra, the friendship of some powerful swimmers
30 against the tide.

---

4 **dedicated** committed, keen – 5 **demand and supply**˙ *Angebot und Nachfrage* –
21 **Oluwole Soyinka** (* 1934) Nigerian literature Nobel Prize winner in 1986 –
27 **inadvertently** accidentally

SIXTEEN

One evening, a man walks into the living room. He makes straight for me and locks me in a powerful embrace. The features come together very slowly. But when he grins I have it figured out. This stranger is no stranger. It is Rotimi, my childhood friend.

5 –Look at this guy.

–How the hell are you?

–What have you been doing with yourself?

–Can't complain. Dealing with this country, and the country's dealing with me. You know.

10 –Doesn't look like it, man. You're looking good. Come here, fool.

We embrace again. His eyes flash like gemstones in the velvety setting of his face. I can't believe it is him, after all this time. And yet it is him, it can only be him, that unmistakable grin. Same

15 as it was when he was a shy five-year-old. Rotimi tells me he is now practicing as a physician. He knows I am training in psychiatry. We just sit there and look at each other in amazement for a while, as if trying to reconcile the image of the children we were with the men we now are. He has his life together, he is a

20 made guy. Purple shirt, silver tie. Very smooth. I grab two bottles of beer from the kitchen. And we sit down and talk. Fifteen years of catching up to do.

–I'm so happy to see you, he says.

–I'm happy to see you too. So tell me, man, what's the scene

25 like here? How's medicine in Naija?

–Ol' boy, it's not easy o. It's not easy at all.

–Yeah, everyone says that. But doctors do better than others, *no be so*?

He loosens his tie and leans back. How quickly time takes

30 hold of us. The diffident kid I knew since I was myself an infant,

---

12 **gemstone** precious stone, jewel – 12 **velvety** soft – 16 **physician** * medical
doctor – 18 **to reconcile** *here:* to connect, to match – 30 **diffident** shy

and here he now is, a man resting after his day's labor. I look at
his hands. In those hands is new knowledge.

–How are the cases?

–The cases are okay, you know. Very wide variety. But it's a
5   private hospital, and they do a pretty good job of keeping it
supplied with drugs, equipment. Well anyway, I'm thinking of
going into pediatrics.

–That's good.

–Should be fine. The kids are okay, actually, it's the parents
10   that are difficult. They're the hardest part of pediatrics. Anyway,
I'll do general medicine for a while yet.

–Yeah, I did my last few rotations in internal medicine last
year. There's a part of me that'll miss that. But the "talking cure"
is a much better fit for me.

15   It is starting to get dark inside the living room, though the sky
is still the color of burnished copper. I switch on the lights. These
Lagos nights that fall without warning: the last glow of day at a
quarter to seven, pitch-black fifteen minutes later. The call to
prayer floats in from the distance.

20   –Well paid?

–Not really. I mean, I live with my parents, so I can manage.
But it's not great.

–What are we talking, a hundred?

–More like seventy.

25   I whistle. Seventy thousand naira a month, for a doctor in a
private hospital. I hadn't expected it to be so little. That comes
to five hundred dollars a month, a pittance. And there's no real
adjustment to make for cost of living because, in Lagos, television
sets cost just as much as they cost elsewhere. This is the reality
30   in an economy that is almost totally dependent on imports. A
used car will set you back ten thousand dollars, same as in the
United States, and a new paperback novel costs fourteen dollars.

---

7 **pediatrics** branch of medicine dealing with children – 16 **burnished** gleaming,
shiny – 27 **pittance**˚ hardly anything, very small amount

Meanwhile, rent is not cheap, and though salaries have risen, they have not kept up with the rate of inflation at all. It is difficult for the average Nigerian to live a middle-class lifestyle. And even those whose profession or education gives them an income well

5 above the average still struggle. And for those in the fifteen-thousand-, twenty-thousand-naira range, life is simply hell. A hundred and forty dollars a month is poverty, anywhere in the world.

–Seventy? So who is making the money? Used to be that

10 doctors were financially well off. Heck, isn't that why our families pushed us to study medicine?

–No kidding. Well, it's not like that anymore. To be a big pawpaw in Nigeria now, you'd better have a job in tele-communications. Or better still, in the oil industry. That's

15 where the moola is. I have friends I went to school with who graduated and went straight into positions that pay three hundred, four-fifty even. Bankers do okay too, two hundred, you know, and more at the merchant banks. But let me tell you, life is hard in Nigeria, man. Life is very hard for the majority. We're

20 all looking to get out. America, London, Trinidad. Wherever.

He stretches out further on the sofa. He looks wiped out. What he says about the economy is true. The oil and gas business rakes in lurid profits, there has been a great increase in cellphone use, and the banking sector is frenetic. The newspapers are full

25 of mergers and acquisitions. These are the limits of the boom. It is good news in the sense that increased commerce is creating jobs, that the economy is active, and certain practical needs of the people are being met. Things are not as stagnant as they were in the dark days of the early and mid-nineties. But there

30 are now more serious discrepancies in income levels, even among people with comparable educational qualifications. There is little incentive for people to go into professions that

---

15 **moola** *inf* money – 23 **lurid** loud, shocking – 25 **merger** ˙fusion – 25 **acquisition** ˙purchase – 32 **incentive** ˙motivation

are not lucrative. Consumption, among those who can afford it, is conspicuous.

We drink. There is much to talk about, and little, as happens when two friends haven't met in a long time. I ask him if it's been a long drive from the island.

–Yeah, really long, man. Why do you say that? Do I look so tired? You have to time Lagos driving just right, getting on the bridge. You leave too late, a forty-minute journey could easily become two hours. Sometimes more.

–That is just crazy. But at least your car is air-conditioned.

–Ha! No chance.

He shakes his head. We look at each other. And just at that moment there is a power cut and we both disappear.

1 **consumption** *Konsum* – 2 **conspicuous** obvious

SEVENTEEN

Rotimi accompanies me to the generator house. In the soot-covered concrete enclosure, we discover that there is just enough diesel in the machine for an hour of electricity. Then darkness until the morrow. I tell him I'm sorry about this. But why, he asks, should you be apologetic? I live in Lagos, I'm used to power cuts. Then he offers to drive me to a filling station. He won't be dissuaded.

The mind roams more widely in the dark than it does in light. It is no surprise, then, stepping out of the unlit house into the unlit compound to find myself with the sudden thought, What if I inhabited another body and had a different destiny? We have all had these notions, perhaps while standing on a porch over a lake in the summer night as our friends enjoy a party indoors, or maybe on waking alone at three in the morning. Moments of great isolation. And there is that other thought: What if everything changed tonight? What if there is an explosion in the generator house? Nighted color seeps into the mind.

The backseat of Rotimi's car, an old Toyota, is full of papers and medical books, including some for foreign exams. I put a large jerry can into the trunk. From the Ojodu–Berger terminus we connect to the Lagos–Sagamu Expressway and travel in the direction of Lagos. After ten minutes, we exit at Ogba and drive to the nearest filling station, but they have no diesel. We drive around that neighborhood, and at the next three stations the story is the same. Either the station is closed, or they are open but have no diesel. Half the city runs on diesel generators, and Nigeria is one of the world's leading producers of crude oil. The shortages make no sense.

Finally, we get back on the expressway, traveling in the opposite direction. In about five minutes we find a place that

---

17 **to seep** to move slowly through material or a hole – 27 **crude oil** Rohöl

has diesel. I am impressed by the way Rotimi talks to the woman at the pump. He falls into a casual vernacular that erases the social distance between them. The message, unmistakably, is that we need her, that it is in her power to help us out. Diesel is
5 advertised at seventy-seven naira per liter. I tell her we want two thousand five hundred worth, and she carefully fills up the jerry can until the numbers on the pump tick exactly to two five. I thank her and pay with a pair of thousand-naira notes and a five hundred. As we pull out of the station and onto the highway
10 Rotimi laughs and says:

–You noticed what just happened, right?

–Um, no. What?

–How much did you pay?

–Two five. That's how much I wanted, and that was the reading
15 on the machine. So don't worry, I had my eye on things.

–Okay, yes, but did you see the advertised rate?

–Sure, it was seventy-seven.

–And how big was your jerry can? Twenty-five liters, *abi be ko*?
20 –Ol' boy, I don't see what you're driving at.

–You had your eye on things! *Omo,* do the maths.

So I do. Twenty-five at seventy-seven only comes to nineteen twenty-five. Christ. She's just had us for almost six hundred naira, easy as that. Rotimi chuckles again and says:
25 –Don't sweat it, that's just the way it is, man.

–This damn country.

Somehow, seeing the advertised rate set into the pump, and seeing the pump tick up the numbers, made me think that everything was clean and official.
30 –We couldn't have done anything about it. That's just the way it is, she has to have her own cut. It saves us the trouble of having to tip her.

---

2 **vernacular** colloquial language – 2 **to erase** *to delete

He laughs again. I am a little annoyed, but I have to marvel at how brazen it all is. So I smile too, and swear again. We cruise on the highway, red lights twinkling directly ahead of us, the white headlamps of oncoming cars flashing to our left. And as we approach Isheri, I say what has been weighing on my mind all evening:

–Rotimi, how did you deal with the, I mean, how did you cope with Sola's death?

The unspoken thing. I haven't seen him since it happened, in 1993. From the late seventies and for most of the eighties we were a close-knit crew. Their mother and my father had gone to school together, and when they'd had us three boys within the space of three years, it was natural that close friendships would ensue. And so, the Bamgbose boys are there in those early photos, my fifth birthday, his brother, Sola's third, someone else's tenth. Sola was the youngest of us three, he was the runt, the one we teased constantly, a rambunctious, happy kid. They were always there with me, as the photos went from black-and-white prints to the washed-out colors of the Polaroids, wearing the same bow ties and ruffled shirts that our mothers made us wear to those parties. The lights of the Lagos night interrupt the darkness of the car at intervals, as though we were passing under scanners. Rotimi's face takes on that guarded, distant look that I know so well. But when he starts to talk, it is clear that he wants to open up.

–It was very difficult. You know, he and I were in the same class, in spite of our age difference.

–I never did know what happened exactly. An accident at that boarding school in Abeokuta, right?

–Yes. We were in SS One. I had just turned fifteen, and Sola was fourteen. He was always one of the youngest kids in class. Anyway, one of his friends, a day student, had brought a car to

---

1 **to marvel** to admire – 14 **to ensue** to follow – 16 **runt** smallest and weakest member of a group (*usu* of animals) – 17 **rambunctious** lively – 30 **SS One** Senior Secondary School Class 1 (~ year 10)

school to impress the boarders with. Which, of course, wasn't allowed. And somehow or the other, the car stopped working, developed some fault. So the boy who brought it gets into the car, and the other boys, there are three of them, start to push the car. They finally get it to start, and the three boys stop pushing. They climb up on the trunk for a laugh. But the boy inside the car doesn't see them do this, and he just accelerates and drives off.

We come off the expressway, and ease the car into the congested bus terminus near the housing estate. Rotimi speaks dispassionately, but the weight of the event is still there in his every word. It is about nine at night. The danfos are still active at the terminus, the bus touts are still crying out, but in fewer numbers than during the previous hour.

–All three boys fell off the car. Two of them did not have a scratch. But Sola somehow slammed his head on the road.

–My God.

–And that evening was weird, you know. No one could tell me what had happened. Everyone knew, but I didn't. I was there in the dining hall, and boys were offering me their seats, serving me larger portions than usual. It wasn't normal. I knew something was up. Eventually, one of the prefects took me aside and said my brother had had an accident, that he had been taken to the general hospital in town. And, of course, my parents came to pick me up the next morning.

–When did they tell you he was dead?

–Not until we got home. It was unreal, you know. Sometimes it is still unreal, that Sola could just die like that. Just gone like that. I was all alone. And that was the last time I was ever in Abeokuta. I transferred to a day school in Lagos the next semester.

---

10 **congested** crowded, blocked – 11 **dispassionate** calm, without passion – 22 **prefect** head boy

We park the car outside the compound and Rotimi switches the engine off. We sit. We hear only the sound of the neighbors' generators.

–To be honest, my mother almost went mad. There was a lot of silence in the house for the first year afterward. It was unbelievably hard for all of us. For each one of us, in a different way.

–I can imagine. And now?

–We're fine. Mostly. They're overprotective, of course, but I understand. Even when I don't want to be too careful, I have to think about them and I force myself to be careful. Just for them if for no other reason. Once I told them I had ridden on a motorcycle. My dad almost slapped me. And, you know, he kind of had a point.

We both laugh. I take the diesel out of the trunk, and wipe my hands on a rag.

–Ol' boy, thank you so much for all this driving around.

–What nonsense. Don't mention it. I'm so happy to see you. It's been too bloody long.

–It was a good time, my friend. Stay in touch, okay? Let me know how I can help. Especially when you decide to take those American licensing exams. Don't hesitate, use my mailing address, have me send you forms, whatever it is. The program I'm in is quite small, but there are always opportunities in New York.

–Most definitely.

He smiles, hugs me as if he were comforting me. He gets into his car and drives away, waving the whole time. And, because it is night, my mind continues to trace alternatives.

29 **to trace** ˙ to find, to outline

EIGHTEEN

The field I am standing in is mostly dust, but it has sere grass
in scattered patches. Six men sit in the shade of a large Indian
almond tree. One of them, a young man in a skyblue cap, is
blind in one eye. For some reason, I keep thinking his damaged
5 eye is rolling over to look at me. It is hot and nobody talks. Ahead,
near the wall that demarcates the field, a black goat grazes. The
grass is so low and rare that the goat kneels on his front legs and
eats in an angled position. He chews at one patch and shifts
around on his knees and eats from another. Head to ground,
10 rump raised in the air, outlined starkly against the off-white
wall, he looks like a plane about to land.

It is a school field but quiet because the children have all gone
away on Christmas break. It is late afternoon. We are waiting for
a container. My aunt built a school on the outskirts of Lagos in
15 the late eighties. She spends all her money on keeping it supplied
with resources so that it can compete with the many other private
primary schools in the city. Uncle Tunde's brother had, in
October, filled up a medium-size container in Chicago and sent
it to Lagos. The shipment contains books, personal effects, and
20 a car. The car is a three-year-old Honda Civic. It is one of the
cheapest of the four-door sedan cars on the American market,
but nonetheless a fine car to have in Nigeria. The container
arrived in Apapa only in the third week of December. But the
field in which we are waiting is not at my aunt's school. This is
25 an older school belonging to their family friend Mr. Wuraola.
They have decided against sending the container all the way
across Lagos. Instead, they plan to off-load the container at Mr.
Wuraola's field in Surulere and then use small school buses to
carry the goods to Ojodu. The reason for this is to avoid attracting
30 the unwanted attentions of hoodlums in the neighborhood, for
whom the sudden appearance of a large container might be an
invitation to robbery.

1 **sere** dried out *(verdorrt)*

There is a Yoruba word: *tokunbo*. That is the term for the secondhand imported consumer goods that flood the Nigerian market. It means "from over the seas." This word is also a Yoruba first name, given to those who were born in foreign countries before being brought back home. That is the primary use of the word, but the other sense, the adjectival one, has become common. *Tokunbo* cars, *tokunbo* clothes, *tokunbo* electronics. A word that was once a mark of worldliness now has a mildly pejorative air about it. The importation of used goods is vital to the domestic economy in Nigeria, as the manufacturing industry is not well developed. But in addition to those goods destined for the market, there has also been a steep rise in imports by private citizens for personal use.

Our wait in the field in Surulere is only the latest in a long series of delays. Already, hundreds of dollars have been spent on bribes and unofficial taxes. The previous day, we received a dressing-down from a customs officer at the port who was enraged that his colleague had left him out of the take. And the container is two weeks late. Two weeks and four hours. Then it arrives. Godot is here, says my uncle. Godot's been rigged to a flatbed trailer, brought through the highways and winding streets from Apapa to Surulere. The trailer pulls into the field. The black goat stops eating and looks up. He gets to his feet and goes away, through the main gate. We don't see him again. The men under the tree get up from their half slumber. The container is opened quickly, and we started unloading it. We begin with the smaller boxes and work in a chain to transfer them from the container into the little vans. Many are schoolbooks for the various grades. Others contain everyday objects like dish soap, parboiled rice, and lamps. Aunty Folake and Mr. Wuraola supervise the work. Mr. Wuraola, with his red T-shirt tucked into his khakis, looks exactly like a middle-aged American.

9 **pejorative** negative *(abwertend)* – 14 **Surulere** residential and commercial Local Government Area located on the mainland of Lagos – 17 **dressing-down** *Schelte* – 20 **to rig** to attach – 22 **Apapa** Local Government Area in Lagos, located to the west of Lagos Island; it contains a number of ports. – 25 **slumber** sleep, nap

When about half of the boxes have been brought down, the driver of the trailer and his assistant set up a winch and an incline. One of the school bus drivers gets inside the Civic and very gently eases it out of the container down into the field. It
5 gleams, looks as good as new compared to the other cars, which have suffered the streets of Lagos. That is when they come in. Three of them. Even from the distance it is obvious that this is trouble. We stop arranging boxes. Two of the drivers immediately go to the far end of the field to meet them and to keep them
10 from getting too close to us. Mr. Wuraola turns to his workers and says:

–How did they get in? How did they get in?

We all look at each other. Our hands hang limp at our sides. Mr. Wuraola paces near the car in his khakis and red T-shirt.
15 Aunty Folake says:

–But what do they want?

Mr. Wuraola says:

–How did they get in? I told you men to keep the gate closed.

–It was closed, sir, says one of the drivers, but it wasn't locked.
20 They must have reached inside and undone the latch and removed the padlock.

The three of them look in our direction and start moving past the men who have gone to meet them. When we are within earshot they stop and one of them raises his voice:
25 –*Eyin ti l'owo, awa naa gbodo l'owo.* You have become wealthy and we must become wealthy too.

Area boys. Unemployed youth in Lagos neighborhoods, notorious for exacting fines and seizing goods. They operate in gangs and report to a godfather. The city is full of them, and no
30 laws of the land or of human decency apply to them. It is also well known that, at intervals, the police murder numbers of

2 **winch** device for lifting heavy loads *(Winde)* – 3 **incline** slope *(Rutsche)* –
28 **notorious**° infamous, having a bad reputation – 30 **decency**° politeness, civility *(Anstand)*

them and deposit their bodies in the lagoon. Every Lagosian has stories about the area boys. It is well known that no one can win an election in Lagos without their support. Mr. Wuraola says softly to my aunt:

5 –They are only after money. What they do is follow the containers all the way from Apapa to wherever they go, and then they demand money. They did the same last year when I brought in a shipment.

Money for nothing. Uncle Tunde is infuriated and he, too,
10 starts pacing near the Civic. The men who have been sent to pacify the area boys come back to us.

–We gave them five hundred, sir. They are asking for more. They say they want fifteen thousand.

More than one hundred dollars, just for walking through the
15 gate. My aunt has no intention of paying, as she has already spent too much on clearing the goods. Her friend agrees with her. And, in any case, no one has that kind of ready money. The area boys can see us deliberating. They start shouting.

–What if we had met you out on the roads? There's no telling.
20 We could have killed you!

–Yes, you're lucky we are here only. Is it too much to ask that you share the wealth? Nobody leaves this field until we are satisfied. You hear that? You hear that? Nobody leaves. We'll do whatever we have to do.

25 –That's right. We'll rip open these boxes and take our share. We will become rich today. We might even take the car. It's a nice car! Or if we don't take it, we can smash the windscreen.

We are silent. They move closer. Their eyes are bloodshot, their chests stuck out. There is tension in the air, a tension in
30 the divide between our bewildered silence and their complete lack of inhibition. Let them open some boxes, my aunt says in

---

18 **to deliberate** to reflect, to think – 30 **bewildered** confused – 31 **inhibition** ˙ nervous feeling *(Hemmung)*

a low and angry voice, maybe they are really into books. We outnumber them almost three to one, counting only the men in our group. And the area boys aren't particularly impressive in stature. But it makes no difference. They are primed to maim or kill as the spirit moves them while, on our side, we have ordinary people who have only the normal instinct for safety. Uncle Tunde says to Mr. Wuraola:

–Can we call the police? I have a phone, let us call the police.

–It's no use. The police will come, sure, but they in their turn will ask for thirty thousand. We'll have to pay double. But don't worry. These guys can't do anything. They are just posing.

I am not so sure. The area boys strut around. They continue shouting. The drivers, desperate to calm them down, go over and give them another five hundred naira. They take it but renew their demand for the fifteen grand. The tension builds, minute gives way to minute. A quarter of an hour goes by. The area boys stop shouting but they continue to pace around the field, eyeing the boxes and the Civic. For some reason, they don't come right up to where we stand. They simply trace a semicircle around us, the perimeter of which they walk back and forth. Something in their movement brings to mind hyenas keeping their distance from a carcass.

We are unsettled. My aunt sits in one of the vans, holds her head in her hand, and quietly begins to cry. I feel like a tuning fork, vibrating with an unfamiliar will to violence. There is nowhere to run to and I have no desire to run. I can no longer bear the violation, the caprice, the air of desperation. If they attack, I say to myself, I will crush their throats. I think of myself as a pacifist, but what I want now is to draw blood, to injure, even to be injured. Crazed by the situation and by the need for an end to it, I no longer know myself.

---

4 **primed** prepared, trained – 4 **to maim** to injure, to cut up *(verstümmeln)* – 22 **carcass** cadaver – 24 **tuning fork** *Stimmgabel* – 27 **caprice** sudden change of behaviour, impulse

And then, as suddenly as they appeared, they leave. They shake their forearms at us, turn around, and head for the gate. We stand stock-still as they open the gate, step out, and close it behind them. The sky darkens rapidly over Surulere. My uncle says:

–Will they come back? Will they wait outside for us?

–Don't worry about it, Mr. Wuraola says. Empty threats. But you know, it would be wise to leave the car here tonight. It's safe in the school compound. Come back and pick it up in a few days. They won't bother us again. They'll take some money from the trailer driver when he leaves, but not too much. He knows it is part of his expense.

We all work at double pace to finish loading the vans. Nobody can avoid the thought that one of the four vans might be waylaid on the way. We agree to drive in tight convoy. My uncle and my aunt enter one of the vans, and I another. I feel sad. This is life too close to the edge of danger for me. It is too severe a tax on the right to private property.

Night falls. The convoy streams out of the school. Each driver nervously looks right and left as we move through Surulere and onto Western Avenue. Finally, out on the open road, we relax. The traffic thickens at Ikorodu Road and we lose sight of each other. The van in which I am riding selects an unfortunate route–we run into a total standstill at Anthony and yet another on Allen Avenue. The fight lies sleeping like a snake in my veins. We do not arrive at Ojodu until two hours after the others.

14 **to waylay** to ambush, to wait for and stop sb to attack them

97

NINETEEN

"One can't say it aloud, but there is a lot of repressed violence here. That is why the furnishings seem so heavy. And why it is so difficult to see the other thing present: a spot of sun that moves over the house walls and slips over the unaware forest of
5   flickering faces, a biblical saying never set down: 'Come unto me, for I am as full of contradictions as you.' "

I pretend for a moment that these lines of Tomas Tranströmer's were written with Nigeria in mind. It is not hard to see how they fit our situation. The contradictions he writes about are the
10 contradictions of poetry, the voice that says: maybe this, maybe that, maybe something else. But in an atmosphere in which the past has been erased, contradictions are forbidden. The typical middle-class Nigerian living room is a dark space. Anchored with weighty upholstery and veiled in thick curtains that banish
15 all light, it announces to all visitors that the household is prosperous. The windows are never opened, the furniture has to be immovable. These are the rules. What is this place? A cipher enclosed within a riddle.

It is late morning, a Wednesday. I wander around old Lagos.
20 There was a brief, sudden shower earlier in the day, the only rain I have seen in these harmattan weeks of my journey. As the downpour began, the congested streets opened up as people fled from one spot to another. The rain in Lagos takes everyone by surprise, regardless of season. The bright heat has now
25 returned. At the artery of the CMS junction, which is always dense with rapidly moving human bodies, my mind makes a heavy and unexpected connection: the secret twinship this city has with another, thousands of miles away. The thought is of

---

2 **furnishings**° furniture – 7 **Tomas Tranströmer** (1931–2015) Swedish poet, literature Nobel Prize winner – 17 **cipher** message in code – 21 **harmattan** a dust-laden wind on the Atlantic coast of Africa (Harmattan season: late-November to mid-March)

the chain of corpses stretching across the Atlantic Ocean to connect Lagos with New Orleans. New Orleans was the largest market for human chattel in the New World. There were twenty-five different slave markets in the city in 1850. This is a secret only because no one wants to know about it. It was at those markets that buyers came to bid on the black men and women who had survived the crossing, but that is a history that is now literally submerged. Actually, it was submerged long before the recent flood, the city's slaving past drowned in drink and jazz and Mardi Gras. High times: the best cure for history. The human cargo that ended up in New Orleans originated from many ports, most of them along the West African shore. And here was another secret: none of those ports was busier than Lagos.

The fratricidal Yoruba wars of the eighteenth and early nineteenth centuries were a great boost to the transatlantic traffic in human beings. There were constant skirmishes between the Ijebus, the Egbas, the Ekitis, the Oyos, the Ibadans, and many other Yoruba groups. Some of the smaller groups might even have been wiped out from history, as the larger ones enlarged their territory and consolidated their power. The vanquished were brought from the interior to the coast and sold to the people of Lagos and to communities along the network of lagoons stretching westward to Ouidah. And they in turn arranged the auctions at which the English, the Portuguese, and the Spanish loaded up their barracoons and slave ships. Some of these intertribal wars were waged for the express purpose of supplying slaves to traders. At thirty-five British pounds for each healthy adult male, it was a lucrative business.

---

3 **chattel** slaves – 9 **recent flood** here refers to Hurricane Katrina (2005) that destroyed much of New Orleans and caused many people to die in the floods – 14 **fratricidal war** war between brothers or members of you own group , civil war – 14 **Yoruba wars** in the 1830s Yorubaland was swept up in these civil wars. New centers of power sought access to fresh supplies of slaves. – 15 **boost** · increase – 16 **traffic** · trade – 16 **skirmish** fight – 20 **vanquished** · defeated, beaten – 25 **baracoons** barracks used for the temporary confinement of slaves

Slave ships visited the river mouths of the Niger Delta, the broad network of tributaries that stretches between Lagos and Calabar, for a period of three hundred years. Here, they needed no forts as they did at Elmina in Ghana or on Goree Island in
5 Senegal. This is because the calm waters of the delta made it possible to berth the ships for weeks or months, however long it took to fill them up with slaves. And because of this geographical peculiarity, little physical evidence remains of the long and bitter engagement. There is little for tourists to see
10 here. According to a memorandum attached to the Report of the House of Commons Select Committee on the Slave Trade in 1848, the trade out of Africa was in the tens of thousands every year in the early nineteenth century, much higher than it had been in preceding centuries. It reached an annual peak of 135,000
15 in the five-year period between 1835 and 1840. At that time, several hundred ships were being loaded up each year along the Niger Delta. And this was in spite of a British ban on the trade in 1808, and a British naval presence in Nigerian waters. According to Alan Burns in his *History of Nigeria,* Spanish,
20 Portuguese, and Brazilian ships often sailed under American colors until they were out of range of the British ships. This history is missing from Lagos. There is no monument to the great wound. There is no day of remembrance, no commemorative museum. There are one or two houses in Badagry that
25 display chains and leg-irons but, beyond that, nothing. Faulkner said: "The past is never dead. It's not even past." But in Lagos we sleep dreamlessly, the sleep of innocents.

These are my thoughts as I visit the famous CMS (now called CSS) Bookshop on Lagos Island. From the arcade of the building
30 that houses it, I can see area boys waving down commercial motorcycle drivers and collecting money from them. Those who resist are rough-handled. Earlier, further up the road, I had seen

---

2 **tributary** ['trɪb.jə.ter.i] river that flows into a larger river or a lake, river arm –
6 **to berth** to dock – 18 **naval** referring to a country's military ships

the police doing the same thing. Police shakedowns, as are also alleged to happen in New Orleans. Our shared sin. In the arcade, someone has spread books out on the ground, and it is as if the bookshop has spilled out of its confines. There is a copy of Samuel Johnson's *The History of the Yorubas from the Earliest Times to the Beginning of the British Protectorate* for sale, but I find it steep at almost three thousand naira. Samuel Johnson, in spite of his name, was Yoruba. He was a peace activist, a priest of the Anglican Church, and a great historian. He wrote his masterly text in 1897. There has not been to date another work of comparable scope by a Yoruba historian.

The interior of the shop is vaguely familiar from my visits here as a schoolboy, when it was the leading bookseller in the city. I used to come here with my mother when there was something we couldn't find at the University Bookshop in Akoka or at the Abiola Bookshop in Yaba. I don't remember the offerings being

---

1 **shakedown** activity of getting money from sb by threatening them – 5 **Samuel Johnson** (1846–1901) Nigerian historian and Anglican priest – 7 **steep** *here:* expensive

as limited as what I see now: the books available for sale are restricted to a few categories. Many of the volumes are dusty and damaged at the edges. There are primary and secondary school textbooks and there are assorted volumes on computer
5 programming, on accounting, and on law. The largest section of all is devoted to "inspirational" and Christian books. While I'm browsing, a woman walks in and brusquely asks the attendant where she can find Bibles. She is directed to a well-stocked section, the only section of the shop in which there is
10 more than one customer. The titles of the books are reiterations of a few themes: how to make money quickly by adopting certain simple principles, how to discover God's plan for your life, how to live a healthy, wealthy, and victorious life according to the precepts of the Pentecostal church.
15   The shelf given to general fiction is small. Other than a few tattered copies of plays by Shakespeare and Soyinka, all that is available is a handful of recently published novels, among them Chimamanda Ngozi Adichie's *Purple Hibiscus* and Sefi Atta's *Everything Good Will Come*. These two are first novels by young
20 Nigerian women based in the United States, and they are here most likely because they have an energetic young Nigerian publisher behind them. There is also a single copy of Dan Brown's ubiquitous book. And I see a stack of books by James Hadley Chase, a minor imitator of Ian Fleming's, who was inexplicably
25 popular in Nigeria when I was growing up and apparently still is. But where are the Nigeria-based Nigerian writers? Where is

---

4 **assorted** diverse – 5 **accounting**˙ bookkeeping – 10 **reiteration** repetition – 14 **precept** principle – 14 **Pentecostal church** evangelical church emphasizing a direct and personal experience with God through the Holy Spirit and the use of spiritual gifts (*Pfingstkirche*) – 16 **tattered** torn – 18 **Chimamanda Ngozi Adichie** (*1977) Nigerian feminist writer who became world-famous for the novel *Americanah* – 18 **Sefi Atta** (*1964) Nigerian author of prose and plays – 22 **Dan Brown** (*1964) American thriller writer, author of *The Da Vinci Code* – 23 **ubiquitous**˙ omnipresent – 23 **Hadley Chase** (1906–1985) bestselling English thriller writer – 24 **Ian Fleming** (1908–1964) English author, journalist and naval intelligence officer, best known for his *James Bond* series

the selection of international literary fiction? The reader I saw on the danfo had surely not bought her book here. Poets, too, are notable by their complete absence.

There is an information desk at the back of the shop. I go there with the idea that I might ask some questions. The woman standing behind the high desk is slumped over, like a large mammal felled by a single shot. But she is not dead, only sleeping, the same as the woman I saw at the museum. A standing fan slowly shakes its large head from left to right to left. It covers her in breezes. What I am looking for, what Tranströmer described as a moving spot of sun, is somewhere in the city. But it is not easy to find, not here where one has to forget about yesterday.

Why is history uncontested here? There is no sight of that dispute over words, that battle over versions of stories that marks the creative inner life of a society. Where are the contradictory voices? I step out of the shop into the midday glare. All around me the unaware forest of flickering faces is visible. The area boys are still hard at work, but I imagine they will soon break for lunch. The past is not even past.

14 **uncontested** not disputed

TWENTY

I left under a cloud. My departure was sudden and, to my family, a complete surprise. Only one of my father's cousins, from whom I had borrowed some of the money for the ticket, had had an inkling about what I planned to do. I had recently finished school
5   at NMS, the military secondary school I attended for six years. I made up an excuse to stay behind after that final semester, while I put my plan into action. Five years previously, I had darkened a doorway in our house in Ikeja and watched my father lie in bed, weak from tuberculosis.
10   My father's death opened up the final cavern between me and my mother. The deprivations of life at boarding school became my refuge. It was better to be there with those military brats, to struggle for survival in that Darwinian environment, than to sit in a large and silent house with my mother and her oppressive
15   grief. Our relationship, never good to start with, got markedly worse in those years. I spent long vacations with my uncles and aunts and, by the time I entered my final year of secondary school, I knew I had to leave Nigeria. When she got my letter from New York, in August 1992, she wrote me back. Her letter
20   was full of alarm and questions. Why have I done this thing? When do I plan to return? Why do I act without thinking through the consequences? I read it once and ripped it up. I never wrote her back. I needed to restart my life on my own terms alone. And that has been the limit of our communication since then,
25   a commitment to silence that, even now, I am surprised I was able to keep up. My communication with those who remained at home was almost as bad, not out of any ill feeling, but from the need to make the break complete. There were also the pressures of remaking my life in the new place. Uncle Tunde

---

4 **inkling** suspicion – 11 **deprivation** deficit – 12 **brat** unpleasant child that behaves badly – 15 **markedly** noticeably – 20 **alarm** panic

wrote to tell me my mother had left Nigeria not long after I did, that she had moved to California. He included the information on how to find her if I wished to. All my time in the United States has been on the East Coast and in the Midwest: New York, Wisconsin, and, for the past several years, back in New York. She, as far as I know, is still on the West Coast. We will not meet accidentally.

In this journey of return, the greatest surprise is how inessential her memory is to me, how inessential I have made it, even in revisiting sites that we knew together, or in seeing many people who knew us both. People know better than to ask about her. This is what it is to be a stranger: when you leave, there is no void. Mother was a stranger here. She left no void after eighteen years, as if she had never been here. And I, fatherless, am also like a man without a mother, even if it is her face and her pale color that looks back at me from every photograph and reflective surface. I roam all over Lagos, and even once travel along the road that links Unilag with Yaba bus stop, but I cannot bring myself to revisit the site, along that road, of my father's grave, at Atan Cemetery.

In December, dust drowns the city. But one Friday morning in the third week of the month, it rains heavily for only the second time in the dry season. It is a relief. It makes the roads torturous. Where there were shallow depressions, lakes suddenly appear. Rivulets rage along the roads. The rain falls for an intense half hour just after I head out. On Allen Avenue, through the gray scrim of the rolled-up windows, I see a swarm of lime-green shirts and yellow trousers, lime-green blouses and yellow skirts: students caught in the rain, racing for shelter. These teenagers, thrilled by the weather and by the excitement of running together, are laughing, but are inaudible through the heavy rain drumming on the car roof. I drive slowly through this dream of hurrying bodies.

13 **void** ° emptiness – 25 **rivule**t stream

The rain stops as suddenly as it started. The city is becalmed and devastated as it always is after a downpour. The streets are clear, the air renewed, and I only have to avoid some puddles as I turn off Ikorodu Road. I'm on my way to visit an old friend.

5 I'll call her Amina. She's a woman now, the same age as I am, but when I last saw her, she was a girl and I was a boy, and we'd just come past the moment of first love. Our love, a matter of months, has remained with me all these years as one of my few sweet memories of the city. Recently, through email, we found

10 each other again. We didn't talk about the past, but now I am on my way to visit her.

Near Akoka, on a road I know well, a police officer flags me down. Lean, in a black uniform, with a hungry look, he walks toward the car. His gait is that of a much larger man, a capacious

15 and considered saunter. His colleague, equally lean, doesn't get up from their makeshift shelter, which is set back from the road: a bench, four wooden poles, a tin roof. It's a sniper's hideout.

–Good afternoon, Officer.

–You know why I stopped you?

20 His certainty alarms me. No, I say evenly, I don't know.

–What does that sign say?

He points to a sign behind us. Its upright element is bent, and the sign itself is partially obscured by a tree.

–Oh God. I didn't see it. This road never used to be a one-way.

25 It must be a new sign.

It's a scam, of course. The sign has been deliberately concealed.

–It's one way from here to the end, until the entrance to the university.

–I didn't know. Sorry. I didn't know.

30 He chuckles. The moment has been well rehearsed.

–This is not a matter of sorry.

–I didn't see the sign. I didn't know.

---

14 **capacious** big – 15 **considered** careful – 15 **saunter** walk – 16 **makeshift** improvised – 17 **sniper**˙ sharpshooter – 23 **obscured** hidden – 26 **deliberately**˙ intentionally

–The sign is not for those who know, *oga*. The sign is for those who don't know. Your situation is unfortunate. But the reason the sign is there is for you. You have to come to the station with us.

5 Minutes are wasted. I don't want to let go of my entire afternoon only to later pay a "fine" that will end up in someone's pocket. Finally, he comes around to his demand, or rather, he compels me to make it explicit.

–So, what are we to do now, Officer? Maybe one thousand five 10 hundred, so you can get yourself something to eat?

His opening bid is five thousand naira. I manage to hide my disgust, and bargain him down to two thousand five. I hand the money over, start the car. You people should know the law, he says. It doesn't matter who you are, the law is not a respecter of 15 persons.

I keep my eyes on the road. My face floods with fury.

Amina has come out onto the street to meet me. She looks like herself: girlish still, slender, with chubby cheeks. She wears her hair in an afro usually, but today she's plaited it simply. I 20 catch sight of her wounded hand (a kitchen accident), which she makes no effort to conceal. Three fingers, two stumps. I back into the driveway of the two-story duplex. It's a middle-class home, a ground-floor apartment of, I guess, two or three bedrooms, with exterior paint that has gone gray in parts. Air 25 conditioners protrude from several windows and, from somewhere, comes the hum of a generator or two. In the doorway is a man whom I suppose is her husband. He carries a sleeping toddler.

–My husband, Henry. My daughter, Rekia. Please come in, 30 come in.

We are playing grown-ups.

---

8 **to compel** to force – 18 **slender** slim – 18 **chubby** round – 19 **to plait** to braid –
22 **duplex** house made up of two flats or housing units – 25 **to protrude** to stick
out – 28 **toddler** small child, who is learning or has just learnt to walk

Amina's living room has solid red floor-to-ceiling drapes and a hushed air. She looks less girlish now. The interior has brought a seriousness to her mood and her body. I notice the bags under her eyes, little dots of heat rash on her cheeks, and the nubs
5 where her right middle and ring finger used to be. Daylight shoots through in a white column where the drapes fail to meet in the middle. Conversation is polite. Henry is a kind, narrow-shouldered man with the beginnings of a paunch. The flat-screen TV, which is on but muted, is playing a Nollywood drama.

10 He is a banker; he has Friday mornings off. Amina recently left banking and is looking for the next thing. She says she enjoys the opportunity to be with her daughter, but there's something dutiful in the answer. I ask them about their commutes to work, and about whether they plan to have more children. They don't
15 ask me much about myself. They do ask if I'd like lunch, and I say no. She has, I presume, told him about me: the first heart she broke (or perhaps it was the other way around). It would be different if I was alone here with her, without the stranger who knows nothing of our conversations, our letters (belabored
20 cursive on perfumed paper; where are they all now?), our long-ago truancy, our first frightened moments in bed, the shame and delight after. And then doing it again and again, any opportunity we had, swept up in a hunger like none since.

The pauses last too long. The tension is that of a waiting room,
25 and I wonder why I have come, why I have chosen, yet again, to recover the impossible. I tell them about my encounter with the policeman, careful not to sound too angry about it.

–You see what we have to face in this country? she says, laughing. But you paid too much. One thousand naira would
30 have done it.

I listen closely to her laughter. I can't quite reconcile it with what I remember. I can't tell if it has darkened or if it is some

---

1 **drape** curtain – 4 **heat rash** small red spots on the skin caused by heat *(Hitzeallergie, Hitzeausssschlag)* – 8 **paunch** belly – 9 **Nollywood** nickname referring to the Nigerian film industry – 21 **truancy** * absence from school without permission *([Schule] schwänzen)*

other difference. Is there some trace in her every reaction of that day her hand was caught in the food processor? There had been a power surge, a mutual friend had told me. Something had slipped, somehow, or she had reached into the machine. The blades had whirred, and she'd lost a lot of blood.

I'm distracted by this thought when Henry asks me something.
–Sorry?
–I said, Did you think you could move back here?
–Oh, who knows? The money would have to be right.

Things would have to fall into place. It's easier for bankers than for doctors. We have good banks and bad hospitals.

Another pause. Traffic outside. Generators. There are many lives and many years, and relatively few moments when those individual histories touch each other with real recognition.

At no time is Amina awkward in handling objects. It is she who gives me the glass of water, in the clawlike grip of her right hand. When she writes (but this I know only from hearsay) she writes with her left. She had to learn again, with a hand different from the one that used to write to me. On the television, the camera zooms in on a man with wide eyes, then cuts away and zooms in on another man, with whom he's locked in staring combat. The little girl finally wakes up. Hello, Rekia, I say. She shies away.

Amina says:
–So moving back has crossed your mind?
–It has crossed my mind.

This is the answer I have heard others give. It will be many weeks before it rains again. When I leave their house, I wipe water from the side-view mirror to get a better glimpse of the three of them waving me bye. They are close together and small, as in a medallion of the Holy Family.

3 **surge** sudden increase

TWENTY-ONE

I escape family and go out into the city on my own to observe its many moods: the lethargy of the early mornings, the raucous early evenings, the silent, lightless nights cut through with the sounds of generators. It is in this aimless wandering that I find
5 myself truly in the city. The days go by. I do not delve, as I had thought I would, into my childhood, do not visit my former schools or look up other old friends.

One afternoon, a few days before Christmas Day, as I walk on Allen Avenue with no particular destination in mind, I happen
10 on a sign for a jazz shop. I follow the arrows and enter a small room at the back of a building. Here at last is something that caters to the tastes of the minority. All that is available at the many street-side record shacks is Nigerian music and records by popular black American and Caribbean artists: hip-hop,
15 dancehall, reggaeton. The interior, covered in glass cases and mirrors, is like a miniature version of the set for the final fight scene in Bruce Lee's *Enter the Dragon*. The glass cases have a decent selection of music. There are the "smooth jazz" artists with their cloying offerings, but there are also many discs by the
20 giants: Miles Davis, Thelonious Monk, Sonny Rollins, and many others. The modern jazz adventurers such as Vijay Iyer and Brad Mehldau are also well represented. The ceiling of the shop is, like all the walls, a mirror. The reflective surfaces, in combination with the bright fluorescent lighting, have the peculiar effect of

---

2 **raucous** loud – 5 **to delve** to dig – 9 **to happen on** to see accidentally – 12 **to cater to** to serve – 17 **Enter the Dragon** a 1973 martial arts action film produced by and starring Bruce Lee – 19 **cloying** too sweet – 20 **Miles Davis** (1926 – 1991) very famous and influential Afro-American jazz musician – 20 **Thelonious Monk** (1917 – 1982) highly influential Afro-American jazz pianist – 20 **Sonny Rollins** (* 1930) jazz tenor saxophonist, very important and influential jazz musician – 21 **Vijay Iyer** (* 1971) American jazz pianist and composer – 21 **Brad Mehldau** (* 1979) American jazz pianist

making the room feel not bigger but, rather, smaller and weirder, as if one were stuffed into one of those camera obscura boxes so favored by the early Dutch lens grinders.

A woman and a man are talking at the cashier's table when I come in. The woman is also working on an accounts book. I look around the shop, and when I have taken note of what is available, I ask about prices.

–Oh, sorry, none of it is for sale.

–Excuse me?

–The compact discs are not for sale. Unless you want to pay three thousand five for each one.

I am confused. A jazz shop, but the discs are not for sale. Unless I pay twenty-five dollars for each, an absurd figure. Most of these discs wouldn't cost me any more than fifteen dollars in the States, and some of the reissues would be considerably less. What could be her meaning?

–But, sir, if you see something that you like, what we can do is make a copy for you. That applies to any disc in the shop. And that costs one thousand naira. But the originals are not for sale.

A legitimate business, with a public sign, on one of the busier commercial streets in town, catering to a sophisticated clientele, and all the while living on piracy. Do they have any idea that this is a problem? Or is it enough to settle for sophistication without troubling oneself about the laws that defend creativity? The following week, I visit a shop called Jazzhole on Awolowo Road in Ikoyi. And there I finally find myself in an inspired and congenial setting. The place is a combination music and book shop. The owner is one of a small but tenacious breed of Nigerian cultural innovators. The presentation is outstanding, as well done as many a Western bookshop: there is a broad selection

---

3 **lens grinder** *Linsenschleifer* – 15 **considerably**˙ very much – 20 **legitimate**˙
legal – 22 **piracy**˙ theft – 27 **congenial** pleasant – 28 **tenacious**˙ firm – 28 **breed**˙ type

of jazz, Pan-African, and other international music near the capacious entrance, and rows and rows of books for the general reader toward the back. The shop has a cool and quiet interior. Here, I think to myself, is finally that moving spot of sun I have
5 sought.

I see music by Ali Farka Touré, by Salif Keïta. There are books by Philip Roth, Penelope Fitzgerald, and, as I had hoped, Michael Ondaatje. The prices are high; not higher than they would be in an American or British shop, but certainly beyond the reach of
10 most Nigerians. And yet, knowing that there is such a place, in the absence of good libraries or other vendors, makes all the difference to those who must have such sustenance. And better at these high prices than not at all. But the illegitimate business model of the other jazz shop is a threat to this essential work.
15 The people behind the bookshop have also created a record label–they have released three albums by the wonderfully named highlife artist Fatai Rolling Dollar–as well as a publishing house. One of their newest projects, the book *Lagos: A City at Work,* is a huge textual and photographic compendium of the life of labor
20 here. It features the work of Nigerian thinkers, writers, and photographers, all grappling with the "nonlinear nature" of the city. It is a brilliant confrontation with our great behemoth of a settlement. And there is really only one word for what I feel about these new contributions to the Lagosian scene: gratitude.
25 They are emerging, these creatives, in spite of everything; and they are essential because they are the signs of hope in a place that, like all other places on the limited earth, needs hope.

---

2 **capacious** large – 5 **to seek (sought, sought)**˙ to try to find – 6 **Ali Farka Touré** (1939 – 2006) also called "Bluesman of Africa" – 6 **Salif Keïta** (* 1949) one of the most respected afro-pop singers of his generation – 7 **Philip Roth** (1933 – 2018) famous American novelist – 7 **Penelope Fitzgerald** (1916 – 2000) English Booker Prize–winning novelist, poet, essayist, and biographer – 12 **sustenance**˙ food – 17 **Fatai Rolling Dollar** (1927 – 2013) Nigerian musician, described as a "nationally celebrated performer" – 22 **behemoth** [bɪˈhiː.mɑːθ] monster, giant

TWENTY-TWO

I am in the van with Aunty Folake and Uncle Bello. They have many errands to run and I've come along for the ride. Every moment I can spend with them is a pleasure. My aunt is a devout Christian who gets up at five every morning to spend an hour
5   with the Bible and devotional texts before the sun rises. Her brother is a committed Muslim. The group he belongs to is called NASFAT, the Nasrul-Lahi-il-Fathi Society of Nigeria, the major Islamic renewal organization in Lagos. With his placid temperament, he is the very antithesis of a jihadi, which makes
10   it funnier that his sister and brother-in-law sometimes tease him with the name Mr. Osama. But, as far as I can tell, they never actually discuss religion, much less attempt to convert each other.

    We have several stops to make this morning: we have to buy
15   some live chickens, we need to refill some large jerry cans with palm oil, and there are repaired suitcases to pick up from the leather worker. So we drive all around the neighborhood and I get to see how thickly populated even these outlying areas of the city have become in my absence. Out here, at the spreading
20   edge of the gigantic metropolis, there is a feel of busy village life. It is an urban density, but in the rhythms of certain interactions, away from the highways and major bus stops, life is languid, and the general feeling less frenetic.

    The woman selling the oil expertly measures out the exact
25   amount required. The fluent substance is beautiful to watch. It falls in an orange-colored cord from one vessel to the other, gleaming in lines like twisted silk. Across the street from where

---

2 **to run errands** * to go out to do things (e.g. shopping, appointments, etc.) – 3 **devout** * sincere, serious – 5 **devotional** religious – 11 **Osama** allusion to the terrorist Osama Bin Laden (1957–2011), founder of the militant organisation al-Qaeda and responsible for masterminding the September 11 attacks in 2001. – 12 **to convert** * to try to change sb's opinion or faith *(bekehren)* – 23 **languid** * relaxed – 26 **vessel** container

we buy palm oil, there is a long line of children and women fetching water at a tap. They carry brightly colored plastic bowls. They are orderly. The solitary faucet comes out of a pipe attached to the fence of a large private house. But how does this work?
5 My aunt says:

–The government doesn't provide any running water in this area. So you've got a local big man with his own water supply. Borehole, electric pump, underwater tank, overhead reservoir. That whole system. He puts a tap outside his house, hires
10 someone to watch over it, and charges per bucket. Fifteen naira per bucket, payable before you even fill up your vessel.

I see a child of no more than eight place, with great care, a brimming basin on her head. It sits there in quivering balance. She picks her way across the street, one sure foot after the other,
15 and goes into one of the small houses. A life on the margins. For these people who must buy water every day, if there is no money on a given day, it means there is no water that day. And when there is water, every drop is cherished like a quintessence. We drive on. One thought leads to another, as thoughts do, and Ben
20 comes to mind. Ben is a young man attached to my aunt's school by the National Youth Service Corps. I say:

–You know, I quite like Ben.

–Oh yes. He's a good man. Very hardworking, and conscientious. He's Ogoni, you know.
25 –That, I didn't know. Those people have suffered. All that oil wealth, and they don't see a penny of it. Nigeria has been rough on them. Ken Saro-Wiwa hanged, all the military repression, the ongoing environmental damage.

I am warming to my theme. Then my uncle says:

---

3 **faucet** • *Wasserhahn* – 8 **borehole** well – 13 **brimming** full, nearly overflowing – 13 **quivering** shaky – 18 **to cherish** to value – 23 **conscientious** • very reliable *(gewissenhaft)* – 24 **Ogoni** indigenous Nigerian tribe who fought Shell Oil after various oil spills – 27 **Ken Saro-Wiwa** (1941–1995) Nigerian writer and environmental activist who led the Ogoni protests and was hanged by the military dictatorship of General Sani Abacha.

–Awon ko l'o m'an je'yan ni? Aren't they the ones who eat people?

I laugh. Oh, come on, Uncle, come on, I say, why are you Nigerians so fond of rumors? We–and what I mean is you–are so tribalistic sometimes. And anyway, don't our Yoruba people also have some kingship-related and grimly nonvegetarian ritual?

That makes them both laugh. The chickens in the backseat start making a fuss, but they soon quiet down. Uncle Bello says:

–But what rumor? Rumor nothing! Okay, I'll tell you a story about my friend Constance. Constance works at the same company in Agidingbi as I do. This lady is from Ondo State, and she got posted to the Ogoni area for her stint on the National Youth Service Corps. And you should know that she's an *afin,* an albino. Well, during the orientation week, and this was in a fairly remote region, near the tribals and such, there was a racket at the gates every night. This went on for three nights, people singing and howling and rattling the gates late into the night. Until the Youth Service people said, you know, just what is going on out there? So they asked around, and it turns out that there's a belief in this village *pe afin o b'osi rara, won fe fa sita, won fe pa je.* Ah! They wanted the albino brought out to them so they could cook and eat her.

My eyes widen. My aunt chuckles. The particular Yoruba choice of words makes the story even funnier.

–Poor Constance. You better believe she cleared out of there by the next day! She finished service in Lagos, and not long after, she got posted to my company.

And then he adds:

–So be careful around that Ben. You just never know when the guy might be hungry.

Such a terrible story, and we are all in stitches the rest of the way home.

---

12 **stint** short or fixed period of time – 15 **racket** noise – 31 **to be in stitches** to laugh so hard that your sides hurt

TWENTY-THREE

At times, the absurdity makes one laugh. Other times, the only possible response is a stunned silence. Shortly before I left New York for Lagos there was a plane crash in Nigeria. A Bellview aircraft plying the Lagos–Abuja route went down three minutes
5 after takeoff, into forests near the village of Lisa in Ogun State. None of the 117 passengers on board survived. A government inquiry was promised, and there was much public hand-wringing and talk about a time of national prayer. While I am in Nigeria two months later, a plane belonging to Sosoliso
10 Airlines goes down on the Abuja–Port Harcourt route. One hundred and eight people are killed, and there are two survivors. The victims include seventy-five schoolchildren returning home for the holidays. Almost all of them are pupils of the Ignatius Loyola Jesuit boarding school. Many of the parents witness the
15 accident, because it happens on arrival, when the plane overshoots the runway. The fire department has no water, and can only watch as the plane incinerates its passengers. There are harrowing scenes of parents contending over the bodies of children burnt beyond recognition. A few days later mothers of
20 the dead children stage a peaceful protest in Lagos. At the march, these mothers, some of whom lost as many as three of their children, are teargassed by police, and that is the end of the matter. There is no further protest, and there is no redress.

A phrase I hear often in Nigeria is *idea l'a need*. It means "all
25 we need is the general idea or concept." People say this in different situations. It is a way of saying: that's good enough, there's no need to get bogged down in details. I hear it time and again. After the electrician installs an antenna and all we get is

---

2 **stunned*** speechless – 17 **to incinerate** to burn – 18 **harrowing*** upsetting – 18 **to contend** to fight – 23 **redress*** compensation – 27 **to be/get bogged down** to be so involved in sth complicated that you can't do anything else *(sich in Einzelheiten verlieren, verzetteln)* – 27 **time and again*** repeatedly

unclear reception of one station, CNN, instead of the thirty pristine stations we had been promised, the reaction isn't that he has done an incomplete job. It is, rather: we'll make do, after all *idea l'a need.* Why bother with sharp reception when you can
5 have snowy reception? And once, driving in town with one of the school drivers, I discover that the latch for the seat belt is broken. Oh, pull it across your chest and sit on the buckle, he says, *idea l'a need.* Safety is not the point. The semblance of safety is what we were after.
10 Around the time the second plane goes down, I am planning a journey to Abuja from Lagos. I think I can take the chance, but no one else in the family agrees. I buy the ticket anyway, and fly less than a week after the plane crash. I have great faith in the laws of statistics. But on that flight, I ask myself: When
15 was the last time two commercial flights went down in the same country within six weeks of each other? And if two, why not three? The Nigerian situation is special. There is reasonable cause for fear. Nigeria Airways, the national carrier, went defunct after years of mismanagement. In its stead, foreign airlines ply
20 the lucrative routes between Lagos and Europe. A number of private ventures supply the flights within Nigeria and West Africa. There are several flights each day between Lagos and Abuja. But Africa, which accounts for less than four percent of the world's air travel, is where more than a quarter of all plane crashes occur.
25 The official inquiries into the Nigeria crashes reveal that many of the private airlines use old planes. Some of these aircraft have been in service for over thirty years. They are *tokunbo* planes, bought after they had been discarded by European carriers. This is a recipe for disaster in Nigeria's poor-maintenance culture.
30 Another serious part of this problem is corruption. The aviation authority failed to enforce a recommendation that all planes older than twenty-two years be removed from service.

---

8 **semblance** similarity, *short for* resemblance – 18 **to go defunct** to no longer work, *here:* to go out of business – 31 **aviation*** flight – 31 **to enforce*** to make sure that a law is obeyed

Had that recommendation been followed, the recent disasters might have been averted. As it stands, there is little doubt that substantial bribes have changed hands to keep the old planes flying. On the day of my outbound flight, the government 5 grounds Sosoliso and Chanchangi Airlines. The ban is lifted shortly afterward. On the day of my return to Lagos, all Boeing 737 planes in the country, regardless of airline, are grounded. This leads to long delays at the airport. There is no explanation from Virgin Nigeria when we finally board our flight, six hours 10 late.

Nigeria's situation brings to mind the cargo cults of Melanesia who cleared runways in the forest and constructed "control towers" out of bamboo and raffia in the belief that these structures, parodies of modern aviation, would bring material 15 blessings from the sky gods. Much like these Pacific Islanders, Nigerians do not always have the philosophical equipment to deal with the material goods they are so eager to consume. We fly planes but we do not manufacture aircraft, much less engage in aeronautical research. We use cellphones but we do not make 20 them. But, more important, we do not foster the ways of thinking that lead to the development of telephones or jet engines. Part of that philosophical equipment is an attention to details: a rejection of only the broad outlines of a system, a commitment to precision, an engagement with the creative and scientific 25 spirit behind what one uses.

Abuja, Nigeria's capital city, rises out of the Sahel like a modernist apparition. The avenues are clean and broad, and the government buildings are imposing, with that soulless and vaguely fascistic air common to capital cities from Washington, 30 D.C., to Brasília. The National Mosque is a gigantic sci-fi fantasy,

---

2 **to avert** ° to prevent, avoid – 5 **to ground** to prevent from flying – 11 **Cargo cult** superstitious belief system among members of an undeveloped society hoping that various ritualistic acts such as the building of an airplane runway will result in the appearance of material wealth – 26 **Sahel** transition zone from the arid Sahara (desert) to the north and the belt of humid savannas to the south – 27 **apparition** phantom, spirit, ghost

like a newly landed alien mother ship. The National Cathedral, a spiky modernist confection, is nearing completion. These houses of worship, in competition with each other for prestige, are two of the most prominent buildings on the city's skyline.
5 The Thai restaurant to which my friends take me for dinner is as tastefully appointed as any I have seen elsewhere in the world. It is also far more expensive than most Nigerians can afford. The bowling alley we go to afterward has neon lanes, thumping music, and fashionable young people. But are these the signs
10 of progress? Yes, partly. Business is booming, there is free enterprise and, with it, the hope that people might be lifted out of poverty.

But it is as yet a borrowed progress and it is happening in the absence of the ideological commitments that can make it real.
15 The president of the Federation is unable to get away from constant God talk, and in this he is very much like his constituents. President Obasanjo's hobbyhorse is the "image"

---

2 **spiky** sharp, pointed – 2 **confection** a work of fine craftsmanship – 17 **constituent** [kənˈstɪtʃ.u.ənt] *here:* voter

of the country. He believes that the greatest damage to Nigeria is being done by critics. These unpatriotic people are, in his opinion, the ones spoiling the country. He insists that the only real flaw is in the pointing out of flaws. One should only say good things. After all, no society can claim perfection.

While the buildings and roads of the capital city suggest a rational, orderly society, the reality is the opposite. Supernatural explanations are favored for the most ordinary events. Uncle Tunde told me a story about his father, who had passed on a few years ago, a jovial, chain-smoking fellow that I met twice as a child. For years, the old man never went to bed without having a half-pint bottle of his favorite tonic: the stash of Guinness Stout that he kept hidden under his bed. He eventually died peacefully in his sleep, at the impressive age of 106. But after his death, there were still family members who muttered that someone must have used black magic on him. *W'on se baba yen pa ni:* someone did the old man in. Nothing happens for natural reasons. There's a widespread belief in the agency of magic and malefaction. In addition to this animism is the recent epidemic of evangelical Christianity that has seized the country, especially in the south.

Church has become one of the biggest businesses in Nigeria, with branches and "ministries" springing up like mushrooms on every street and corner. These Christians are militant, preaching a potent combination of a fear of hellfire and a love of financial prosperity. Many of the most ardent believers are students in the secondary schools and colleges. This is the worldview in which prayer is a sufficient solution for plane crashes. Everyone expects a miracle, and those who do not receive theirs are blamed for having insufficient faith. Partly in response to this, and partly from other internal urgings, Islam has also become extreme, particularly in the north. Some of the

---

4 **flaw·** fault, mistake – 12 **stash** supply – 17 **to do sb in** to kill sb – 19 **malefaction** lawbreaking, evil deeds – 19 **animism** belief that all plants, animals and objects have spirits – 26 **ardent·** eager

northern states, such as Zamfara, are de facto theocratic entities in which sharia is the law of the land. Staying opposite the Zamfara State House in Abuja, I could not sleep for the constant wailing emanating from the official mosque in the compound.

5   Nigeria's disconnection from reality is neatly exemplified in three claims to fame the country has recently received in the world media. Nigeria was declared the most religious country in the world, Nigerians were found to be the world's happiest people, and in Transparency International's 2005 assessment, 10 Nigeria was tied for third from the bottom out of the 159 countries surveyed in the corruption perceptions index. Religion, corruption, happiness. Why, if so religious, so little concern for the ethical life or human rights? Why, if so happy, such weariness and stifled suffering? The late Fela Kuti's prophetic song 15 "Shuffering and Shmiling" still speaks to the situation. This champion of the people was also the fiercest critic of the people. He spoke fearlessly to our absurdities. "Shuffering and Shmiling" was about how, in Nigeria, there is tremendous cultural pressure to claim that one is happy, even when one is not. *Especially* 20 when one is not. Unhappy people, such as grieving mothers at a protest march, are swept aside. It is wrong to be unhappy. But it is not necessary to get bogged down in details when all we need is the general idea.

---

1 **theocratic entities** areas where religious leaders rule – 2 **sharia** Islamic law – 4 **to wail** to howl, to cry – 4 **to emanate** to come from – 6 **claim to fame** *Anspruch auf Ruhm* – 9 **Transparency International** international organization fighting worldwide corruption – 10 **tied** ˙ *unentschieden* – 14 **stifled** suppressed – 14 **"Shuffering and Shmiling"** 1977 album by Nigerian Afrobeat composer, bandleader, and multi-instrumentalist and civil rights activist **Fela Kuti** (1938–1997); The album is an attack on various non-native religions slowly taking control of the people of Nigeria, causing factions to emerge and rendering the people unable to unify as they would need to.

TWENTY-FOUR

The Ojodu–Berger Bus Terminus is connected to the expressway by a steep dirt road. Hundreds of buses and cars cross at this narrow point every hour, much like a great herd fording a brook and clambering up the opposite slope. Driving south from there,
5 the old toll gate into Lagos is only ten minutes away. On a day when the traffic is light, it does not take long to pass by the districts of Alausa and Oregun. From the high bridge at Ojota, where the length of Ikorodu Road stretches into the city as far as the eye can see, one has a panoramic view of the thickly
10 populated area below: cars, molues, danfos, people. Perpetual movement. It is familiar. When we lived in Opebi, I traveled the route hundreds of times as a child on school-day mornings. Now those hundreds of journeys come to mind as if they were a single vivid one. Ahead, a gigantic recumbent woman purrs from a
15 billboard, "Who are you sleeping with tonight?" It is an advertisement for a mattress manufacturer. Next to it is another billboard, featuring young people dancing at a party. The tagline: "No wonder Nigerians are the happiest people on earth." The sponsor of the billboard is British American Tobacco.
20 As we pass Ojota, I see something else, set in a low plain to the right, just off the expressway. There are high walls with ramparts that mimic a medieval castle. Inside, visible from the road, is a dense cluster of buildings surrounding a busy parking lot. At the entrance of the complex, there is a soaring red gateway:
25 Chinatown. Chinatown in Lagos? But there it is, another signal that we are in a normal place, or a place that aspires to normalcy, like New York, London, Vancouver, San Francisco, with their Chinatowns. This one fits the bill, right down to the giant Chinese

---

3 **to ford** to cross – 4 **to clamber** to climb – 14 **recumbent** declining, resting –
22 **rampart** dirt wall – 24 **to soar*** to rise – 26 **to aspire to** to seek – 28 **to fit the bill**
to fit perfectly, to match

characters on the frontage. The Chinese have arrived, and they are visible all over Lagos, as merchants, as contractors, as laborers. This is home to them now. They established the Chinatown complex in 1999, selling bales of cloth, consumer
5 electronics, digital media, kitchenware. Nigerians come in droves, for the cheap prices. But it isn't an easy life for the Chinese. The merchants have terrible difficulties at the Nigerian ports bringing in their goods. They have to pay hefty bribes, and delivery times are erratic. And, while I am in Lagos, the state
10 government temporarily shuts down all the shops in Chinatown, on the pretext of investigating a compact disc piracy ring.

But not only the Chinese are new to the city. People from all corners of the world have come to take advantage of the newly open economy. Indians, Lebanese, Germans, Americans, Brits.
15 I see them in the restaurants, in shopping malls, at the open markets. They have their own private schools, their own housing remarkable, always subject to stares from adults and cries of *oyinbo* from little children. Other Caucasians were few and far between, clustered in Ikoyi and on the campus of the University
20 of Lagos. That has changed now. There is a lot of money to be made in Nigeria, and the world in all its colors is here to make it. The self-described "giant of Africa," closed for so long because of its reputation as a difficult place, is now open. There is now all this activity, as pent-up energy is released, and people are
25 driven by a sense that business is possible. But the past continues to gather around like floodwater. A too easy formulation, but what past do I have in mind? The nation's, I think. But perhaps I am also thinking of mine, perhaps the two are connected, the way a small segment of a coastline is formed with the same logic
30 that makes the shape of the continental shelf.

The car ahead of us in traffic, a decrepit Peugeot 504, has a sticker featuring a smiling face and the words "Relax! God is in control." It occurs to me that the barely concealed sense of panic

---

1 **characters** what we call letters are characters in Chinese – 2 **contractor** builder (with his own business) – 4 **bale** large roll *(Ballen)* – 6 **droves** masses – 9 **erratic** unreliable, random – 24 **pent-up** repressed

that taints so many interactions here is due precisely to the fact that nobody is in control, no one is ultimately responsible for anything at all. Life in Nigeria, in Lagos in particular, requires constant vigilance. It is entirely possible to put on a happy face,
5 but what no one can really do is relax. A story my aunt tells me brings this home. They had had two dogs, a sleek basenji called Zo and a temperamental bitch they named Maryam Abacha, in honor of the then-dictator's wife. The dogs died, on the same day. My aunt says that sometimes, before robbers attack a house,
10 they kill the guard dog by throwing poisoned treats over the fence. She thinks it unlikely that their dogs had both succumbed to natural causes: they must have been poisoned. I ask her when it happened. "It was just a few days before you arrived," she says. I wonder if this means we are due another visit by the armies
15 of the night. The possibility is too terrible to contemplate out loud.

The sight of the empty kennels with their rusting wires unsettles me in a different way. Not fear: it is something much less distinct than that. The feeling lasts through the weeks. It is
20 there as an undertow during the various reunions with friends and family. It is intensified by the sobering sights I see as I roam around the city. Struggle and absence. A dizziness, here among the happiest people on earth. In Nigeria we experience all the good things that texture a life, but always with a sense of
25 foreboding, a sense of the fragility of things. But what if everything that is to happen has already happened, and only the consequences are playing themselves out? That is more troubling still. I have to pass by those kennels each time I come into or leave the compound. They are built right next to each
30 other, set into the concrete walls around the house. They cannot be removed or banished into memory, and the way they sit open now makes them look emptier than when they were new and unoccupied.

---

1 **to taint** to smear, to stain *(beschmutzen)* – 6 **Basenji** hunting dog bred in Africa –
21 **sobering** * *ernüchternd* – 25 **foreboding** * premonition *(Vorahnung)*

TWENTY-FIVE

The proliferation of new eateries designed on the American fast-food model surprises me. When I left in the early nineties there was just one, Mr. Bigg's. Now there are several, many of them operating on the franchise system, in every neighborhood
5 of the city. Mr. Bigg's and its main competitors–Tantalizers and Sweet Sensation–are well-run establishments serving pastries, burgers, and Nigerian specialties. In general, these restaurants are as clean as the average McDonald's; they are air-conditioned and they have functioning toilets. The increased competition
10 over the years has helped lower their prices. Mr. Bigg's started off as a place for the rich to take their kids, but most of the eateries are now priced to cater to the middle class. It is a modest triumph for free enterprise, a small example of something that is being done right in the new Nigeria. To date, none of the big
15 American fast-food chains has opened in Lagos. Their absence is not felt.

There is a Tantalizers restaurant not far from my relatives' home. Filled with a craving for their peppered snails and stewed spinach with melon seed, I slip out of the house and hire a
20 motorbike to take me there. The motorbike is a good way to get a feel for the city. The commercial motorbike, popularly called *okada* (after the man who introduced them into the Nigerian market), has a justly earned reputation as an extraordinarily dangerous mode of transportation. The passenger has to hold
25 on to the driver's waist as he weaves rapidly through traffic, and the two (or sometimes even three) riders absorb into their bodies the shock from every rut in the road and a coat of the city's fine red dust. Accidents are common. For women, it is too dangerous to ride sidesaddle, so they hike up their skirts to the middle of
30 their thighs and straddle the machine. Many of them wear skirts

---

18 **craving** desire – 27 **rut** *Furche* – 30 **to straddle** to sit or stand with your legs on either side of sth, e.g. on a horse or bike

and traditional wrappers. The motorcycle remains the fastest and cheapest way to travel short distances in Lagos, and even the women do not seem to mind the temporary public intimacies into which it forces them. There have been recurring threats to
5 ban them, but the continuing popularity of the *okada* seems assured.

Riding back from Tantalizers, I see a sign at the side of the road that says: "Bulletproof your glasses." I think at first of Clark Kent, then it dawns on me that it is an advertisement for
10 reinforced car windshields. Other signs, put up by churches or herbalists, promise more biological and altogether less likely miracles: "Expect a miracle tonight," "You will be cured of AIDS and infertility." And it does seem that, nightly disappointments notwithstanding, most people do continue to expect miracles.
15 When I get home, I take a bucket and fall straight to preparing my bathwater. In this season, the minimum number of showers one must take in a day is two. Most days I take three or more, to combat the heat and wash the dust off my skin. The cooling water and the dark bathroom impart an immediate feeling of
20 deep well-being. The thin armor of dirt lifts. Brown rivulets slither off the body and nose their way into the drain. The world is calm and clean again.

The phone rings as I step out of the bathroom. It is my friend Seyi's mother. I have three books to deliver to her from her son
25 in New York. Mrs. Aboaba is a distinguished lawyer at a firm on Victoria Island. But these are not law books: Tony Judt's *Postwar,*

---

1 **wrapper** colorful garment *(Kleidungsstück)* widely worn in West Africa by both men and women – 4 **recurring** repeated – 8 **Clark Kent** Superman's undercover personality – 9 **it dawns on me** it occurs to me – 11 **herbalists** people who believe in the healing power of herbs *(Kräuter)* – 13 **infertility** childlessness – 14 **notwithstanding** aside *(unbeachtet)* – 21 **drain** plughole – 26 **Tony Judd** (1948 – 2010) British-American historian specializing in European history. *Postwar* deals with the history of Europe after WWII.

Samantha Power's *A Problem from Hell,* and an odd completion to the trio, Lynne Truss's *Eats, Shoots & Leaves.* Mrs. Aboaba thanks me for bringing the books for her.

–Do you want to describe the address for me, *ma*? I should
5 be able to bring the books round toward the end of this week.

–Oh no, we won't do that. Too far. I don't want to inconvenience you. I'll send someone to pick them up.

–You're sure, *ma*?

–Yes, that's what we'll do. Are you home this afternoon? Give
10 me your address, I'll send someone from my office to your place.

The doorbell rings an hour later. The man at the gate wears a long-sleeved shirt punctiliously tucked into his pleated ted trousers. He has a slight figure and sharp facial features. He is fair-skinned, and my guess that he is Ibo is confirmed when he
15 introduces himself as Chinedu. I welcome him into the compound and usher him to the living room upstairs.

We sit at the dining table and make small talk. He took the danfo across town, via the Third Mainland Bridge. It was an easy journey, he says, as the morning rush hour was over and the
20 afternoon traffic jams hadn't started yet. I ask if he would like something to drink and he nods. He must be in his late twenties but, save for one rotting tooth, he looks much younger than that. He still has the air of a schoolboy. I notice that he is impressed–the smile gives it away–when I serve him a can of
25 Pepsi. Only then does it occur to me that because canned soft drinks cost much more than bottled drinks in Nigeria–the opposite of what happens in the United States–the can must seem to him an extravagance. I do not want to watch him drink,

1 **Samantha Power** (* 1970) British-born Irish-American author, political critic and diplomat. *A Problem from Hell* is concerned with the history of genocide in the twentieth century and the role the United State has played in it. – 2 **Lynne Truss** one of Britain's best-loved comic writers; wrote the world-wide bestseller *Eats, Shoots & Leaves* in which she bemoans the state of punctuation in the United Kingdom and the United States. – 6 **to inconvenience** to cause problems or difficulties for sb –
12 **punctilious** exact – 12 **pleated trousers** *Hose mit Bügelfalte* – 12 **ted trousers** trousers designed by Ted Baker – 22 **save for** except for

but there is nothing else to do. He sips from a glass. Then, to make it clear he is not a mere messenger, he says:

–Actually I'm a law clerk. I went to university actually. Not one of the big guys at the office, not at all, but we do help out with the filing and some research.

And they are also made to run assorted errands, but he doesn't say that. His manner is shy, but one can see that this is an adaptation. There is a natural volubility in him, something that is being reined in. I want to ask him whether he has a wife, children. I wonder what additional burdens are being carried on these frail shoulders. But I decide against asking. He says:

–Actually I should be getting back.

He hasn't finished his drink. I put Mrs. Aboaba's books in a plastic bag and hand them to him. We walk outside. It is a cloudless day, and the concrete finish of the compound is white in the sunlight. Our shadows bob in front of us. Chinedu begins to sweat right away. I do not perspire as easily, but the cool sensation I had got from my shower is gone. We walk slowly toward the gate, past the open, empty kennels, and as we walk, I thank him. He smiles broadly and says "actually" again, but then he stops and thinks about how to phrase what is on his mind. His eyes are bright. He says:

–I don't want to cause any, I don't know, any trouble.

–No trouble at all.

–What I mean is, I don't want my boss to be displeased with me. So, if possible, you don't have to tell her–

I nod and assure him that I don't intend on sending any reports to his boss. I tell him to feel free to say whatever he wants.

–Well, the thing, sir, is that I am so happy to meet you. I have always heard about people who went over there, you know, to America. But I have never been chanced to meet one. So this is a good day for me.

---

5 **filing** collecting data – 8 **volubility** liking to talk a lot and confidently – 9 **to rein in** to control – 11 **frail** easily breakable, weak – 16 **to bob** to move

He pauses and searches my face, still smiling. Then he goes on:

–Actually I want to know you. I mean, actually, to have us know each other, you know. Maybe one day, by knowing you, I can have a chance to go to America. To know each other, actually, just as friends.

He reminds me of Leonard Bast in *Howards End*. The acute awareness of a social gap and the hope, yet, that the gap can be bridged by enthusiasm and application. He reminds me, painfully, of myself, of times when I was the one in socially asymmetrical situations, in my early years in the United States, the times when I had been someone else's Leonard Bast. There had been that vague humiliation of knowing one deserved better. And here are millions who, justly or otherwise, feel they deserve better. We reach the gate. I unlatch it.

–I understand that. I hear what you're saying.

–Oh, sir, I am so glad you understand, actually. As I said, I am happy to know you. If we could exchange telephone numbers, you know, just to stay in touch. Or your email contact. If you are okay with that.

–Yes, I'm all right. The thing is, Chinedu, I still have to come to Mrs. Aboaba's office before I leave Nigeria. So no rush. I'll see you then, you know, we can exchange information then. Because this phone in my hand now belongs to my aunt. So later will be better.

–Okay, okay. Actually that's good. I hope to see you there. I'm there every day.

–And don't worry. I won't tell your boss. Thanks again for coming to pick up these books. See you soon?

–Yes, oh yes. Thank you.

I shake his hand, knowing full well I will never see him again. He is still grinning, the pearly rows interrupted by that single

---

7 **Howard's End** novel by E. M. Foster published 1910. One of the protagonists, **Leonard Bast**, is a poor insurance clerk at the very bottom of the middle class and constantly worries about money. – 32 **pearly** white and shiny like pearls

derelict incisor.[1] He makes as if to say something else, but he
changes his mind. Nodding, smiling, without further words, we
wave each other goodbye. He begins to walk down the long,
quiet stretch of unpaved road that leads to the gate of the estate.
5 In a few minutes he will be at the bus terminal and once again
join that great mass of the deserving, those countless others
awaiting miracles. He keeps to the center of the road, walking
at an even clip. I watch him for a long time, and his figure
gradually becomes insubstantial as the little clouds of dust take
10 over. After a while, there is only the road.

1 **incisor** front tooth

TWENTY-SIX

I spend three days in a feverish haze, and by the time the twenty-seventh of December arrives, a Tuesday, the date printed on my return ticket, I am in bed in agony. I am hot, cold, hot, huddling in near nakedness under a heavy swathe of blankets, sweating
5 and shivering, my joints hurting. The large dose of Coartem I take seems to temper these symptoms, but it has terrible side effects. I vomit a great volume of liquids, mostly the oatmeal I had for breakfast. And I have to run repeatedly to the toilet to void liquid shit, the body frantic in its attempt to clear itself of
10 the pathogen. I take thalazole to control the stools, mefloquine for the malaria. I hear footsteps, heavy breathing, the sound of a blade edge being worked on stone, the dull flapping of a greatcoat. At the most delirious moment, I think: He's come for me. But the thought flits past, and so do the hallucinations.

15 A guest comes to the bedroom in the late morning. Oluwafemi is a friend from my days in Zaria. He was a junior student to me. Like almost all the other young people I haven't seen in well over a decade, he has grown to imposing size. He is a lawyer in training and is ambitious to someday open a corporate law firm
20 in Lagos.

–I have malaria.

–Oh, I don't say that.

I am puzzled.

–But what do you mean? I have malaria.

25 –I mean I don't say things like "I have malaria." The tongue is very powerful, you know.

–Oh. Well, that's fine and dandy. But the thing, old man, is that I actually do have malaria. So I do say that. I've been sick as a dog for the past twenty-four hours.

5 **Coartem** anti-malaria medicine – 9 **to void** to empty – 10 **pathogen** [ˈpæθ.ə.dʒən] *Krankheitserreger* – 10 **thalazole, mefloquine** names of medication – 27 **fine and dandy** *schön und gut*

–It's saying it that makes it so. You're not sick.

I don't really want to argue with him. At that point, I hurry to the water closet to relieve a sudden urge. When I come back, crawling back into bed, I say:

5 –The female *Anopheles* mosquito has caught up with me. That's the reality. It's the plasmodium parasite denaturing my red blood cells that makes it so, and the sooner I admit that to myself, the sooner I can start treating the disease, Oluwafemi. There's no point in being counterfactual.

10 I search his face, in vain, for signs of comprehension. He only shakes his head, as if he feels sorry for me, stuck as I am in a scientific view of the world. "Relax! God is in control." And in his attitude, I find a key to much of what I have observed in the preceding weeks. The idea that saying makes it so, that the laws

15 of the imagination matter more than all others. But of course, Oluwafemi is vindicated: he is in the pink of health, and it is I, careless of tongue and lacking in faith, who lie under the clammy sheets.

The illness is still in my body when I arrive at the airport for

20 departure. I am feverish, not at all eager to travel. I consider canceling my flight. The officer checking me in asks, rather morosely, if I have anything for him. Dollars perhaps, or naira. No, I say, showing him my palms, I am empty. My bags are searched and, found free of contraband, tagged. They are picked

25 up by a cheerful baggage handler. Anything for him, he wants to know, anything at all? No–nothing tonight, nothing. I go through security and head to the gate. From the plate glass of the terminal, a line of great phosphorescent lamps shines through the dusk, all along the wider tunnel in the main building,

30 until we come to the gate and enter the narrower, enclosed tunnel, and board the aircraft. I buckle myself into the seat.

---

3 **urge**˙ impulse – 9 **to be counterfactual** not to accept facts – 16 **vindicated** free from blame, proven right – 16 **pink** *here:* best – 17 **clammy** damp – 22 **morosely** in a bad or unhappy mood – 24 **contraband** illegal imports

Droplets rapidly form and evaporate on my forehead. All around me, the bustle of departure, people with too much carry-on luggage, disputations over seating assignments. Jets of dry air hiss out of the overhead nozzles and there is a feeling of compression in the cabin. The word "home" sits in my mouth like foreign food. So simple a word, and so hard to pin to its meaning. We have not left yet, and already there is something drawing me back to this city, this country. After the plane is filled, and everyone is sitting and buckled in, and all the overhead compartments are closed, we are stalled on the tarmac for half an hour. And then, at last, and with no explanation from the flight staff, we begin to move. I place my head against the small window.

The plane sheds ballast and rises above the city, rises above the countless small dots of light that are scattered like stars across the landscape, rises slowly into the cloudless harmattan night, easing the compression, rises deep into the ether, until there is nothing visible in the darkness below except for the earth's dark curve.

1 **to evaporate** verdunsten

TWENTY-SEVEN

Snow is total. It robs the street of details and muffles the goings-on outside the window. In the warm interior of the apartment, my body is still responding to the difference in time zone. It is five in the morning. I have insomnia. I hold a cup of tea in my hands. And, as I sit there, a memory of Lagos returns to me, a moment in my brief journey that stands out of time.

I am there again, in the area around St. Paul's Anglican Church, Iganmu, where colonial-style buildings crumble next to makeshift roadside shacks, and the unkempt façade of the Government Press building faces the shiny glass doors of a Mr. Bigg's. Here, the city becomes as trackless as a desert. It is a hot Thursday afternoon. People are hard at their work, and I alone wander with no particular aim. On house after house is painted the straightforward but nonetheless intriguing directive: "This house is not for sale." Little streets wind in upon each other like a basketful of eels; no two run parallel. Losing my geographical bearings in this way always brings ambiguous emotions. Not knowing where I am exposes me to various dangers, and there is always a possibility that I will be accosted by a hostile party. On the other hand, letting go of my moorings makes me connect to the city as pure place, through which I move without prejudging what I will see when I come around a corner.

I am in a labyrinth. A labyrinth, not a maze: I hadn't really thought about the difference before, but it has become clear. A labyrinth's winding paths lead, finally, to the meaningful center. A maze, in contrast, is full of cul-de-sacs, dead ends, false signals; a maze is the trickster god's domain. When I enter a little sun-suffused street in the heart of the district, I sense an intentionality to my being there. It feels like a return, like a center, though it

---

4 **insomnia** sleeplessness – 9 **unkempt** messy – 14 **intriguing** exciting, stimulating –
16 **eel** *Aal* – 17 **bearings** orientation – 20 **moorings** anchor

is not a place I have ever been before. It is an alley, and it is full of boats. The boats are in storage. Their prows jut out from the bottom floor of each of the buildings on one side of the street. The buildings are mostly two or three stories high, and the alley
5 itself is no longer than 150 yards. Because the sun is high and I am disoriented, I cannot really tell if this is the street's south side or its north. Across from the buildings, there is a concrete wall behind a stand of three large trees. The wall runs the length of the alley and, underneath the trees, there are young children
10 playing. A woman cooks beans in a large basin. This side of the street is dappled. As I move, or rather as I am pulled, into the little street, as one might be pulled by the broad strength of a receding tide, I see that the jutting shapes are not boats at all. They are coffins, dozens of them, in different sizes and various
15 states of completion, presented in sober and matter-of-fact array.

There are no cars parked on the narrow street, just one or two motorbikes. But there is a lot of activity. Men, bare-chested or in white singlets, work wood with saws, planes, and other carpentry tools. Their bodies glisten in the half shadows of the
20 shops. There are so many of them, it must be a kind of carpentry consortium: this is evidently where they do all their work and live with their families. But their only product, as far as I can see, is coffins. No chairs, tables, wardrobes, or anything else. Only coffins, some painted white, some stained to a lustrous
25 finish, many others pale and as yet unstained. A few wide planks rest on the wall across the street. A darkly polished casket lies on a trestle. It is grand, with brass handles, and looks as out-of-place and unsurprising as a Rolls-Royce parked in a ghetto. It is half-open, revealing a tufted interior encased in plush white
30 satin: an invitation to sleep.

---

2 **prow** [praʊ] front of a ship, bow – 2 **to jut out** to stick out – 11 **dappled** speckled *(gefleckt)* – 13 **to recede** to withdraw, to go back – 15 **array** display – 18 **singlet** sleeveless shirt – 24 **stained** dyed, coloured *(gefärbt, gebeizt)* – 24 **lustrous finish** shine – 26 **casket** chest – 27 **trestle** type of frame – 29 **encased** wrapped, covered

I want to take the little camera out of my pocket and capture the scene. But I am afraid. Afraid that the carpenters, rapt in their meditative task, will look up at me; afraid that I will bind to film what is intended only for the memory, what is meant
5 only for a sidelong glance followed by forgetting. A tall man in a sky-blue cap rhythmically moves his arms back and forth over a butter-colored plank. His arms are lean and black, and he has one eye closed as he works. The shavings fall in a nest about his feet. He is ankle-deep in that soft wood-stuff which, I suddenly
10 remember, was so fascinating to me when I was a child of seven or eight. I remember the carpenter who made our furniture, the pile of shavings in his shop, and the sweet, oily fragrance they emanated, an aroma that fit the playful nature of the material, those buoyant curls of gold that seemed to transcend the timber
15 that originated them.

There is a dignity about this little street, with its open sewers and rusted roofs. Nothing is preached here. Its inhabitants simply serve life by securing good passage for the dead, their intricate work seen for a moment and then hidden for all time. It is an
20 uncanny place, this dockyard of Charon's, but it also has an enlivening purity. Enlivening, but not joyful exactly. A wholeness, rather, a comforting sense that there is an order to things, a solid assurance of deep-structured order, so strongly felt that when I come to the end of the street and see, off to my right, the path
25 out of the labyrinth and into the city's normal bustle, I do not really want to move on. But I know, at the same time, that it is not possible for me to stay.

The children cry out from the shadowed side of the street as they play with an old bicycle wheel. One toddler, left out of the
30 fun, begins weeping, until a sibling sweeps him up and tickles

---

2 **rapt** absorbed – 13 **to emanate** to send out – 14 **buoyant** ['bɔɪ.ᵊnt] light – 16 **sewers** *Abwasserkanal* – 20 **uncanny*** mysterious – 20 **Charon** ['kærən] in Greek mythology, Charon is the ferryman of Hades who carries souls of the newly deceased across the rivers Styx and Acheron that divided the world of the living from the world of the dead.

him and he gurgles with delight. The woman keeps stirring her beans, putting a finger in to taste them. This is the street to which the people of old Lagos, right across the social classes, come when someone dies. They come with great fanfare if it is
5 an old person, order the most expensive casket in celebration of a life, hire out the football field of a secondary school, throw a large party with canopies and live music and colorful outfits. But if the deceased is a youth, fallen before the full fruition of life, the rites are performed under grief's discreet shadow, a
10 simple box, no frills, a small afternoon burial on a weekday, marked by bitter and unshowy tears, and attended by neither the parents nor by the parents' friends, for the old should not see the young buried. The carpenters, I am sure, have borne witness to all this. And there are, perhaps, women in the back
15 rooms of their humble houses who help prepare the bodies for their last journey, washing down what remains of a father or mother or child, fitting the heavy limbs into new clothes, putting talcum powder on the face, working coconut oil into the hair and scalp.

8 **deceased** ˙ dead – 13 **to bear witness** ˙ to witness, to watch – 15 **humble** ˙ modest, small

Maps

Map of Lagos

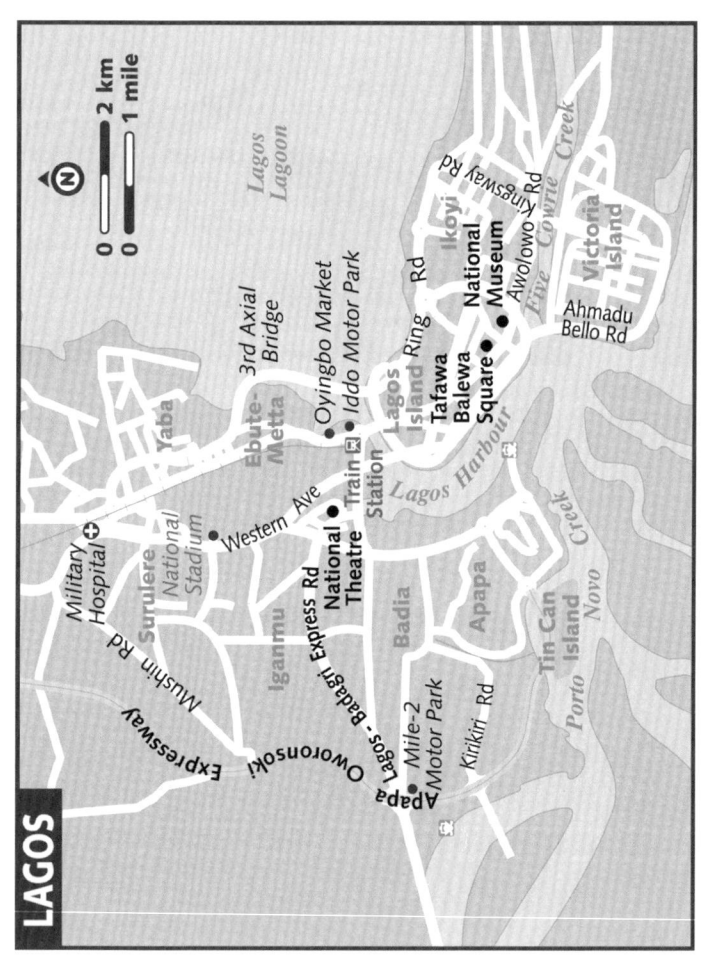

142

Political map of Nigeria

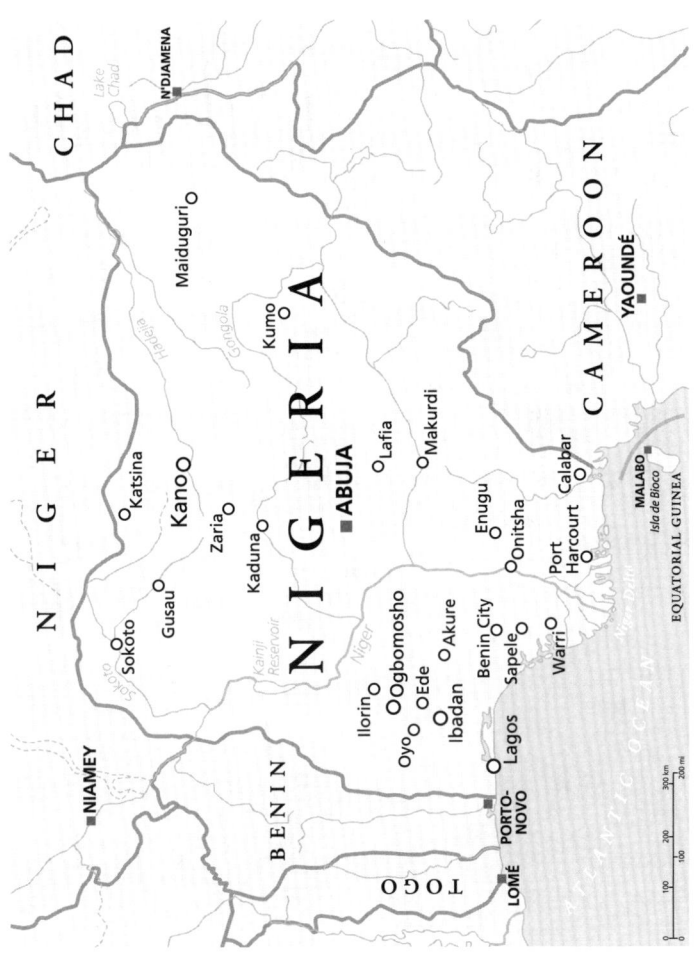

Map of principal linguistic groups

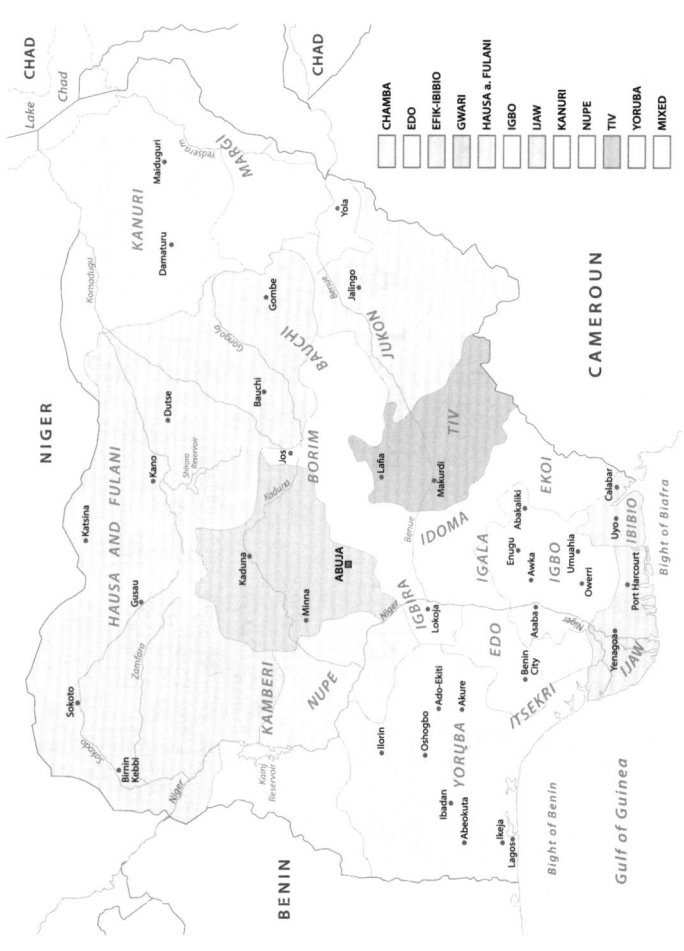

© Shutterstock (Rainer Lesniewski), New York